PTSD
and What
Helped Me

PTSD

and What Helped Me

A step-by-step guide to start your
PTSD recovery journey

SIMONE SWARTZ

ISBN: 979-8-89694-447-8 - Ebook

ISBN: 979-8-89694-448-5 - Paperback

ISBN: 979-8-89694-449-2 - Hardcover

LEGAL DISCLAIMER

The information provided in *PTSD and What Helped Me* is based on the author's personal experiences, insights, and work as the founder of a nonprofit providing service dogs to survivors of sexual assault-related PTSD. This book is intended for informational and inspirational purposes only and is not a substitute for professional medical, psychological, or legal advice, diagnosis, or treatment. Readers are encouraged to consult qualified healthcare professionals, such as licensed therapists, psychiatrists, or medical providers, before implementing any strategies discussed in this book. It is not intended to serve as a substitute for professional medical advice. Always seek the advice of a qualified healthcare provider with any questions you may have regarding PTSD or any other mental health condition. Do not disregard professional medical advice or delay seeking treatment because of the information contained in this book.

Trigger warning

PTSD and What Helped Me contains discussions of sensitive and potentially distressing topics, including sexual assault, military sexual trauma, post-traumatic stress disorder (PTSD), intimate partner violence and drug and alcohol addiction. These subjects may be triggering for some readers, particularly those with personal experiences of trauma, abuse, or addiction. Please engage with this material at your own pace and prioritize your mental and emotional well-being. If the content feels overwhelming, consider seeking support from your mental health provider.

PTSD and What Helped Me
By, Simone Swartz

This book is dedicated to my three babies, my children… my loves. To the ones I held in my arms from your first day on earth and who I still hold in my heart, to where time and space cannot keep us apart. I will always love you no matter what, no matter what happens or what anyone says. From the beginning you three beautiful souls gave me the drive to want to create a better life for us. Mommy loves you till the end of time, until the end of this life and the start of a new timeline. Time, space or people can't keep us apart. The love I have for you will never end. When anyone tells me I am a strong person, I think to myself, not as strong as my babies. Thank you three for being the catalyst to my search for success and healing. You three were my reason to show you and the world that adversity doesn't have to end your dreams. Adversity can be the starting point for your pursuit of a happy and healthy life. Keep God and determination first and never quit. You three will always be my greatest creation.

*"The more you love yourself
the faster the healing comes"*

TABLE OF CONTENTS

Along with this book comes an accompanying workbook! It mirrors each chapter from 'PTSD and What Helped Me', and helps guide you on how you can put into practice the healing solutions directly into your life, as well as journaling exercises. The free digital download link can be found on my website: www.ptsdandwhathelpedme.com

The physical workbook is available for purchase if you would rather have a hard copy. Happy journaling and healing!

CHAPTER 1

Intro

Hello fellow Survivor! I wrote this book to outline the steps I took that helped me get to a better place in my life. This journey took many years, many tears and endless amounts of time devoted to research and self-discovery. After a decade of living with undiagnosed PTSD, then another decade learning to heal from the diagnosis, I finally found hope and healing. To be in a place today where I can speak to others about my trauma and not be crippled by PTSD symptoms is a victory in self resilience and determination. Now that I have completed all the steps outlined in this book, I see how my journey could have taken much less time to complete. Years of struggle and searching could have taken a speedier route if I had the information compiled in front of me when I started the dive into processing my trauma. I hope my stories and life references resonate with you and help you along your healing path. Use the steps I took and therapies as a guide. Reading a book is not a substitute for you doing your own internal work, nor a replacement for seeking help from a medical professional but this book and the steps outlined can be a guide to help alleviate anxiety and confusion about where to start or what to do next when you have set your mission to manage your PTSD.

Recovery is possible. You are stronger than PTSD. You are stronger than the circumstances that caused it. You deserve to live a full life and a life without fear. People with PTSD are strong, not weak. PTSD is not a sign of weakness, it is proof of survival. The fact that you are here seeking answers shows your strength. We Survivors have made it through some horribly difficult situations and are still standing today. That's how I know you can make it through the aftermath as well. You can and will overcome what is hindering you from succeeding. I don't have to meet you to know you're going to be able to live a better life after PTSD and trauma. Why? Because I know PTSD first hand. I am not a doctor or professor quoting studies-I have lived with PTSD. I have also chosen to slowly make changes that have created a happier life for me today. There was a time when I believed I would always be "damaged" but I realized healing comes from taking action. I have come from avoiding my pain and PTSD by the use of drugs and other negative behaviors, to speaking about recovery and peace on a national scale.

Ironically, I would have never gotten such a blessing and experienced all the great progress in my life if I had given up and accepted the thought that I was always going to have PTSD and be "damaged." My desire to live happier and healthier came from a push to overcome the obstacles of

PTSD. If speaking to a group of women with SA-PTSD or sharing the news about my story would get me a step closer to accepting what happened to me and turning it into something positive, then I would do it. When you help others it can be healing to you as well.

Sometimes the aftermath of trauma and PTSD can become more painful than the trauma itself. PTSD can feel like an unrelenting cycle, but you do not have to live in its grip. You have a choice-to focus on change or to let past trauma control your life and future. Reliving the trauma each day does not have to be your choice anymore. We have the choice to focus on prosperous survival or on the addicting feelings of depression which can lead to deeper and deeper lows each day.

Keep in mind that the trauma didn't take you out. You are a SURVIVOR. You have been given the gift of another day. You now have to purposefully start to choose life over depression. Your new life can turn from surviving with PTSD to thriving with PTSD. Although you will never forget what has happened to you, the more you purposefully intend to create positive moments in your life, they can outweigh the negative.

I know your strength because you took action to improve your life today. *You have completed the first and most important step, the decision to want to make a change for the better*. Being fed up with reliving the trauma, avoidant behaviors that try to block out the trauma will leave you stuck on a hamster wheel. We as PTSD Survivors can hold the power of our happiness in our own thoughts. We can't change the past but we can take steps to improve our future.

There will be happy days ahead. Whether your trauma was caused by someone else, or your trauma was losing someone dear to you, I can promise you that no loved one would want you to suffer more than you already have. The person(s) who may have inflicted harm upon you would most likely not care if you were dead or alive, happy or sad. Your misery from their injustice and harm is only hurting you the longer you stay stuck in PTSD-land and don't attempt to find freedom after the pain.

Making a decision to improve your life and symptoms is solely up to you. No one else can control you now that you are more aware and open to healing. The cliche' for *thriving* will be different for each person. Individual goals and levels of PTSD are different so do not compare yourself to others. Imagine right now your ideal life once your PTSD symptoms are better managed. What does thriving look like to you in six months? What things do you want to accomplish in a year? In two years? What are the main symptoms hindering your everyday life that you want to change and improve?

This book details my personal journey and steps that I took to improve my life and PTSD symptoms. Keep in mind that I am not a medical professional. I am not a counselor. This book is not intended to be medical advice, diagnosis or treatment for any disease. Consult your doctor and mental health care team before implementing any new therapy into your treatment plan. I always encourage that you please find a counselor you're comfortable with and who can encourage you to change and not stay stagnant.

I am an ordinary person who has experienced some extraordinary pain and trauma in my lifetime. I was able to find a roadmap that worked for me. The healing I have found has allowed me to wake up happy and with a smile. Not because it is free of drama, but because I am free more days than not of debilitating PTSD symptoms. I am truly grateful for each day God has given me when I don't think of my trauma first thing each day or miss an opportunity because of PTSD. I have noticed my trauma not only created more traumas, but I became addicted, in a way, to misery. It truly takes a deep desire to break out of old patterns even when they are harmful. It takes courage to start a new life when you have experienced long term trauma or endured severe violence.

All things are possible when you are fully dedicated to healing and recovery. For each reader, my hope for your life is that you find the ability to keep yourself safe and to flourish. This could mean relearning a different way to live in every aspect of your life, but I know it can be done.

I know that healthy living is possible and much more sustainable than living in fear, anger and addiction.

Freeing yourself from PTSD symptoms was my purpose for writing this book. There are no shortcuts to healing, doing the individual work, self-discovery or learning new healthy behaviors. You are not alone in your PTSD struggle.

I wanted to share my path with a passion because those of us with PTSD are often bombarded with much negativity over having a mental health diagnosis. There is a severe lack of resources for mental health recovery. But there is a lot of self help and you will have to be the one who makes the decision to reach out for help.

The hard facts are that we really have no one to rely on other than ourselves and God. You are going to have to accept the fact that no one is coming to save you. No one is going to do your healing work for you. No matter how much someone is supporting you, the hard work and desire for health must come from within you. You are the only one who must consistently show up for yourself on a daily basis.

Organizations, people, police, courts, friends, family, even counselors all have limitations and flaws which can sometimes cause more trauma onto the PTSD sufferer.

<u>Choosing to see your PTSD as a badge of strength that you are still alive instead of a bag you have to carry everyday will help you slowly change your outlook.</u> PTSD is not a stigma that prevents you from things, but living with PTSD in a healthier, non-self-destructive way will require you to adapt to a new lifestyle. Healthy adaptations you can add into your life will open different opportunities. You may not be able to live your life the way you used to before your trauma, but you CAN still live. Live differently AND live happily. You must be brave and be able to think outside the box. I may not be able to work a typical 9 to 5 job anymore, but after my healing I am able to open my eyes to a different, alternative line of work. Instead of focusing on the jobs I can no longer do, I AM able to write and share my experience at my own pace. This

experience has become a better reality than I could have ever imagined before my trauma.

When I was in high school, I held dreams of becoming a journalist. My father was an international journalist and graduate of Georgetown University. I had a love for writing and wanted to follow in his footsteps. Fast forward through high school and applying for college. I did not have the resources to enter any college but the local community college. I quickly gave up on my dream of being a journalist. The inability to get into a university would eventually propel my decision to join the Army.

My dream to be a writer I gave up on, until I healed from my _trauma_. Fast forward to 2020 and I was blessed with writing opportunities in spite of not having a journalism degree. Because of my trauma my dream of writing was renewed. I was given the opportunity to write about my military career and the nonprofit I founded. God didn't give up on my dream to become an author even when I had. Opportunities emerged that I would have never imagined years ago. God gave me the opportunity to be a worldwide published author because of my trauma and not in spite of it. God had plans for me to turn pain into power and help others on a greater scale. God opened doors that I would never be able to open on my own. God turned pain into purpose. God gave me the writing career I had always dreamt of.

**Don't limit how much your life
can change with recovery!**

We are all unique individuals with different levels of PTSD, so I can't 'guarantee' the same results that I have had. I do know that a Higher Power can make anything a reality. I know that if you want a different life badly enough and work toward it, it will happen. This is not a religious book and if you don't believe in a God, then that is OK. You will be able to use the other suggestions besides those pointing you to a Higher Power. (I will be using the word GOD, as it is the most universally understood term for a higher power. Please note that whatever name you call your higher power: God, Allah, Yahweh, G-d, Spirit, etc. understand this is your personal choice and highly respected). Recovery is the most important goal and a relationship with your higher power will greatly increase chances of success. My trust in a higher power was a tool I used so I included. Don't rule out something that didn't work for you in the past. If something doesn't work, what is the harm in trying again? Try something new and try something over again. Recovery is not for the weak. Too many people *didn't* recover because they couldn't put in the dedication, devotion or hard work and gave up too soon. Too many people just get stuck in being addicted to pain. In reality, they threw in the towel on themselves. Recovery takes a relentless, never-ending strength to want to live a different way. <u>Your desire to want a happier life must outweigh your discomfort.</u>

In order to truly find progress in your healing you are going to have to put the same dedication you had for your addiction into your healing. The same daily dedication to being toxic is going to have to be flipped. *Are you willing to put in a full fledged effort to feel better?*

I am confident you will enjoy reading this book and I hope you use it as a starting point in your healing journey. Today can be the start of a new decision to put yourself first instead of your focus being on your trauma. You can do it, only if you want it. I promise that life can be livable and loveable. Be strong, be courageous and deal with it head on. Take a deep breath. Today's the day. I'm not saying it will be easy and without effort, but the more you dig into your PTSD and chip the layers away, the easier it becomes. Life can get easier as your effort increases and your layers of trauma decrease. PTSD will not win today or keep you from your blessings. Smile. I'm proud of you. I love you and believe in you.

Key Points:

Healing looks different for everyone

Healing takes time and is not a linear process

Healing and recovery are possible

Action is needed for results

Resting and reflection is also action

Mental determination is key to recovery

Congratulations on the first step to deciding to recover!

CHAPTER 2

PTSD

In this chapter we will not define what PTSD is, as I'm sure you already know. I will however tell you how PTSD affected my life personally. If you want medical definitions and medical input on PTSD from people who have not personally experienced it, there are a plethora of books out there from PhDs that will attempt to describe PTSD pathologies. We are much MORE than a diagnosis. Our diagnosis does NOT have to become our personality. My hopes in writing this book were to shine a light on the facts of PTSD, how it shows up in life experiences and leave the reader with first hand experiences that lead to more happiness. Sharing parts of my story is necessary, yet a complete dialogue of every gory situation is unnecessary. PTSD is nasty, but recovery can be very possible and beautiful.

When I was first diagnosed with PTSD, I was totally shocked. I had no idea PTSD could affect me. I didn't know you could get PTSD from other events outside of military combat. I thought everyone had trauma they were trying to hide. I thought trauma was a normal part of life. I thought the only way to deal with trauma was to drink/drug until you couldn't remember it anymore. My outlook on life and the world was very jaded. I never had the information to heal or the education to create a better outlook on life. I had no resilience to trauma because I had been focusing on the trauma itself, not health and wellness.

When I was given the diagnosis of "PTSD" by my counselor, I was then given a place to start learning. I learned about PTSD and the adaptations for survival I had devised for my life over the years that were not so healthy. I sent myself on a self-propelled journey to uncover the truth about PTSD and to search out all treatments possible. I wanted to learn how to be healthy, in mind, body and spiritually. I did not want to drink myself silly to feel comfortable in a crowd anymore. I did not want to live life fearing another attack. I did not want flashbacks to keep me from sleeping anymore. I did not want to keep saying to myself and to God, "Why me?". Sometimes we must ask ourselves, "Why NOT me?". I wanted the anger to stop and my life to be 'normal'. I didn't realize that a new kind of normal would be waiting. I knew I needed to make changes. I knew I could not keep living this way. I had to address the pain. The diagnosis of PTSD was influential in helping me see how trauma can affect you but doesn't have to BE you. The way I was living was hurting me and I didn't realize it until I had addressed my life in therapy. I thought I could have been an alcoholic or just a dummy. In reality, my body and mind were trying to feel better from events that hurt them. I was avoiding the ability to grow in life and was telling myself I was a broken person.

Learning about PTSD and learning about my adaptations for survival I had been living under for years. I sent myself on a self-propelled journey to uncover the truth of PTSD and to search out all treatments possible. I had to address the pain.

I took it upon myself to make my new goal of healing my new healthy obsession. I became obsessed with changing my life from negative to positive. Once I realized I had a diagnosis that could be helped I wanted this change as soon as possible. I wanted to overcome unhealthy behaviors. My goal was to overcome my self-medicating, avoidance, adaptive behaviors and depression. Depression was a side effect of directly ingesting large amounts of alcohol (which is classified on the drug chart as a depressant) and from living unhealthily with no purpose in life. I knew I had to replace old patterns with better ways to live and deal with my trauma. I was just sick of being sick. I was sick of living, avoiding many activities and having anxiety. I was living a 'normal' life on the outside, but dealing with an overwhelming sense of despair on the inside.

I had multiple jobs, I showered daily and dressed well and went to work. Even drinking after work on a daily basis is an accepted occurrence in our society. The inner turmoil and drinking to the point of blacking out to numb my emotions was something many never saw. I could appear 'happy' on the outside especially when drinking, but when the alcohol was gone I was a social recluse. I had trouble sleeping and held severe guilt and internal shame. My self worth was nonexistent. I felt that I had nothing to live for. I hated myself for an attack I never was responsible for in the first place.

Drinking daily is a socially acceptable behaviour, so it is easy to hide inner pain by drinking and no one around you is the wiser. Having one or two drinks is normally acceptable, but if it's drinking to avoid feelings or block trauma, it is not healthy. I would often, if not every time, drink to the point of no return. I relied on alcohol as my sleep aid, therapist, best friend, parent I never had and counselor. Alcohol and drugs were my bandaids when what I really needed was heart surgery. There came a point when I had to face the things most on the outside did not see. I had to face the fact I could not sleep and I could not interact without being intoxicated. I knew there was a better life to be lived. I didn't want to have to be addicted to daily drugs. I really wanted to travel without anxiety, to start a business, or to raise a family and feel safe in the community. I wanted to do something other than drink and just exist to work a job that didn't make a difference. It was a crazy realization when I saw that many if not all of my reactions and behaviors were molded by my trauma. I could withdraw,- or go hard and dangerous. But either way, I was trying to avoid my trauma. Childhood trauma and military sexual trauma made my search for freedom from PTSD strong. I witnessed PTSD destroy many people's lives that were close to me. It was so hard to witness. Yet it was easier to say someone else had PTSD than to admit it myself.

I have experience with SA-PTSD myself, I have lived with someone with combat and C- PTSD and have many friends that were victims of gun violence or lost loved ones due to violence in America. I have noticed we all share very similar PTSD symptoms. Besides experiencing trauma-specific triggers,- (such as having anxiety around someone who looked like the attacker, or men in general, or an Army uniform, or the sound of gun fire), we all have the typical PTSD signs difficulty sleeping, anxiety in crowds, depression, hyper-self reliance, hypervigilance, distrust of authority figures, avoidance OR hyper-activity (to the point of placing yourself in dangerous situations), and holding the feeling that no one understands what you're going through.

PTSD can be acquired in many traumatic ways. It can come from witnessing violence, having violence directly happen to you. America's streets can be their own 'war zone'. Some of us don't have to enlist in the military to experience PTSD. Experiencing sexual assault or molestation can cause PTSD symptoms. One of the most talked about, but least occurring trauma by population analysis, is from being sent to war (Combat PTSD). There is a far greater population living in America that has experienced PTSD from combat on our streets and didn't enlist. Americans have experienced unbelievable amounts of unnecessary trauma from the hands of police and from the needless violence caused by poverty or other gun violence. Whether you have witnessed combat or violence in the USA or another country, the effects of PTSD can be felt.

I feel called to shed light on these under-discussed ways of getting PTSD. The population that has seen combat is much smaller than the population that has experienced Sexual Assault Post Traumatic Disorder (SA-PTSD) and gun violence in America. I don't intend to diminish Combat PTSD as less damaging, but I need to call attention to the greater populations that are not talked about as often. PTSD is a much more common problem than we care to notice. Yet, healing can only come if we first have experience with SA-PTSD.

I have lived with someone who has seen combat and has C-PTSD (*Combat PTSD*) and have had many friends who have been victims of gun violence or lost loved ones due to violence. My friends and loved ones did not have to go to war to be a victim of such war-like trauma. They did not have to even leave the USA. We all share very similar PTSD symptoms no matter how the PTSD was acquired: through combat overseas, or combat in the United States streets. These signs include having difficulty sleeping, anxiety in crowds, distrust and anxiety around authority figures, avoidance or hyper-activity (to the point of placing yourself in dangerous situations), and holding the feelings that no one understands what you're going through.

The Veteran and active duty population of the US is roughly 7 percent of the US population according to the census bureau. The population of US citizens living in high violence areas (those who have witnessed gun violence or know someone who has lost their life to violence) is hard to calculate. But it is safe to say there are high violence areas in every state. There have been many artists and activists who have documented PTSD symptoms from witnessing crime or being victim to or losing a loved one to violence. It is safe to say this US population is higher than 7 percent. Rainn.org reports 1 in every 6 Americans have experienced sexual assault. With the stigma surrounding anyone who reports a sexual assault and the hesitation from survivors to report, I feel these stats of persons who actually DO report their assault, are truly not encompassing the total picture of the population who have been assaulted. I do not want to downplay combat PTSD, but since it already has much light shed on it, I choose to focus on directing attention to SA and gun violence PTSD. PTSD populations from gun violence and SA have much higher numbers than those Americans who have witnessed combat. All are truly unfortunate, horrible situations, but civilians did not sign up expecting to witness violence.

https://safelives.org.uk/news-views/why-mental-health-support-for-survivors-of-domestic-abuse-is-so-vital/of DA is vital - Safrom Savelives.org, they report "Almost two thirds of domestic abuse survivors experience post-traumatic stress disorder (PTSD)—more than twice the rate experienced by soldiers in combat."

https://www.partnersforpeaceme.org/post-traumatic-stress-disorder-and-domestic-violence/

Partners for Peace says, "PTSD is most often associated with soldiers and veterans—related to the trauma associated with experiencing war and life on the battlefield. However, they are not the only people affected by trauma; a startlingly high number of domestic abuse victims and survivors develop PTSD as well. Studies show that the prevalence rate of PTSD among domestic violence survivors is between 31 percent and 84 percent, compared to about 3.5 percent of the general population."

When talking about SA and PTSD, Kaitlin A. Chivers-Wilson from the University of Alberta Sexual Assault Centre says "The US National Comorbidity Survey Report estimates the lifetime prevalence of PTSD among North Americans to be 7.8 percent (9). The lifetime prevalence of PTSD for women who have been sexually assaulted is 50 percent (10). Moreover, sexual assault is the most frequent cause of PTSD in women, with one study reporting that 94 percent of women experienced PTSD symptoms during the first two weeks after an assault (9)."

https://pmc.ncbi.nlm.nih.gov/articles/PMC2323517/

The point is, PTSD is a huge epidemic and highly under diagnosed. No matter what trauma gave you PTSD symptoms, the steps to relief can be the same. PTSD takes lives every day from people's inability or fear to reach out for help. There is help for PTSD. There should never be shame associated with asking for help or having atrocities happen to you.

No one ever asked or deserved to be abused. There is no way to "cure" trauma that has happened to you. You cannot undo what was done to you or unsee what you witnessed. The way in which you process this trauma, the way you view it and recognize when the memories start to bother you, can most definitely be handled and controlled with your dedication to yourself.

You will always hold memories and reminders, but they can become less triggering and much less detrimental. Even after days or years of dealing with your PTSD in therapy, you may have times when your symptoms will spike. On these days, it is perfectly OK to take a day off. Healing can be an up and down journey. Don't let that stop you or keep you from wanting to live another day. Intense feelings should pass when you reach out to your support and give yourself grace to allow yourself to experience these feelings and memories until they subside. Your counselor should be teaching you tools that can help you with those moments that are specifically catered to your learning style and diagnosis.

A lot of these techniques are breathing exercises, body scanning, grounding techniques and what always helps me and what I prefer is physical release of energy. I will bust out a few push-ups, wall push-ups, or go for a walk or run. Or if you're in an environment where you feel uncomfortable doing a push-up or two, a nice way to calm down and release immediate emotion is to tighten your muscles. You can do a body scan of squeezing all the muscles from your head down to your toes or choose specific muscles to tighten like your fists or toes. Hold the squeeze for around 10 seconds or what feels good to you, more or less, and let go. Squeeze and repeat. Some of this will take specific work, one-on-one with your counselor to determine your specific triggers and your specific tells of when you need support. Even practicing this muscle technique randomly and adding some random quick physical activity during the day will greatly help relax your tension and PTSD symptoms.

I could not change the past but I could change my future. My drive to be happy was so great because I did not want my rapist to keep controlling my life. My goal was to overcome my self-medicating, avoidance, destructive adaptive behaviors and depression.

No matter what trauma has caused your PTSD symptoms, the steps to relieving them can be the same. PTSD takes lives every day because of a person's inability or fear to reach out for help. These are needless losses. There is help for PTSD. There should never be shame associated with asking for help or having such atrocities happen to you. No one ever asked or deserved to be abused.

Healing can be an up and down journey. Don't let that stop you or keep you from wanting to live another day. Intense feelings should pass when you reach out to your support and do something actively positive you enjoy. Give yourself grace to allow yourself to experience these feelings and memories until they subside.

You can achieve living a good life after putting in the work to heal yourself. _Recovery is possible_. I share solutions that I have found helpful, but I am not a doctor or medical professional. One should never give up on life. It is important to know that there is always someone who cares for you. We are here on this earth to help one another. Our burdens can turn into blessings in disguise if we work at our healing.

It takes time and hard work to heal from PTSD, especially if you hold multiple deep traumas. That just means your blessings will be that much greater when you make it to the healing side. Never give up! Find your own solutions. Trying many different healing methods was helpful for me. Know that getting discouraged is normal. Also know that what you put out into the universe will be returned to you. Keep fighting. Find one thing positive in your life even if it's that you're given another day. Focus on your future more than the past.

I believe in you. Keep going. Stay strong. Never give up.

Key Points:

PTSD is described as a normal reaction to un-normal situations.

PTSD untreated can set you up for more traumas.

PTSD is acquired from all types of trauma

PTSD is more of an epidemic than the media or others like to portray

PTSD does not have to overcome the rest of your life

Never give up on healing and a better life.

Unhealed PTSD can lead to more trauma

Focusing on how you show up in life is best to maintain a healthy mindset.

CHAPTER 3

Self Story

Let me briefly explain who I am, some life experiences and an overview of my traumas that lead me to a PTSD diagnosis. I share only for educational value and not for shock. I share to let others know they are not alone and to eliminate 'survivor shame'. My intention is to share parts of my story to highlight PTSD effects and highlight the steps I took to recovery. My intention is to show the correlation between where I have come from and where I am now. I hope my story educates through firsthand experience and paves a way for others to not be scared to tell their story.

I am who I am today and NOT what I have lived through. My life experiences have made me wiser, yet, I have purposefully chosen to define myself as who I want to become and how I conduct myself today. I have done my very best to make positive learning moments from the lowest points in my life. I have had to forgive myself and remove society's unhealthy labels from my timeline. No matter where I have been—stay at home mom, nonprofit founder, homeless, addicted—the motivation to keep going and do better has given me purpose through it all. The motivation I have held in my heart is that recovery is possible. What I have been through will not keep defining me but make me a better person.

Childhood

Born in the '80s with bleach blonde hair and chubby cheeks. I was an only child. Not having siblings, I grew up having a strong connection and love for all animals who kept me company. I always felt at ease around animals. I loved catching bugs and anything to do with nature. I loved learning about the many unusual animals from all over the world.

One night at the dinner table while eating a hotdog, I asked my mother, "Where did meat come from?" She explained that it came from an animal. I never wanted to eat meat again because of my deep respect and connection to animals. I strive to eat with the least impact on the planet and animals whenever possible.

My empathy and love for animals was a steady and continuing bright light in my life. I always felt a strong emotional connection to them, be it a random dog I would walk by, one of the family cats or even a caterpillar or bugs I would find in the front yard. The magic and calmness from my connection with animals over my lifetime has been immense. I believe animals do hold amazing calming qualities and can help with emotional regulation. They can be our biggest comfort in times of uncertainty. Animals are so vulnerable and need our protection. My love for dogs and all animals proved to be influential when I would start the service dog nonprofit later on.

I grew up moving around a lot between Florida, Maine and even some time in Chicago, but primarily residing in suburban Maine. School was difficult for me on an emotional and social level but academics came easy to me. I was constantly asking questions and seeking out answers. I wanted more knowledge about the world going on around me. I held an intense need for justice and fairness. I wanted to know more about life and see what really was out there behind all the Maine pine trees. The typical suburban apathy about social issues and injustice lead me to hold a grudge against those who chose to look away from these inequities. My desire for fairness and equality followed me into leading the nonprofit. My need for answers and endless questions was beneficial to me when I needed to find ways to help my PTSD. This book is based on my research and personal journey to find solutions.

Growing up with a single mom and barely knowing my father, I felt somewhat like an outcast in the American landscape of a two parent, upper middle-class town where I grew up. I gravitated toward music as an outlet, which became a huge encouragement to me. Music was a stress reliever. It helped me to decompress and to center me. The first time I heard 2Pac's cassette tape, "All Eyes on Me," I felt like my world had stopped. My ears and heart were overwhelmingly happy when I heard his uplifting beats mixed with lyrics speaking of social justice change. I felt a connection to his words, to the attitude of "me against the world" and fightting the system. Pac's anti-systematic approach was something I had never heard spoken about in that way before, but believed in to my core. I felt personally connected to his music, his fight for change and his lyrics ended up bringing me through many hard times growing up.

Rap music became my escape and my healing. The intricate lyrics fueled my continued love for literature. I had dreams of being an author or journalist. One of my greatest outlets of self-expression in my life has been writing. I encourage anyone dealing with trauma to start writing even if it is to throw away the paper afterward. There is intense healing when you are able to convey your thoughts and emotions on paper. Writing has always been my go-to art form and another reason I resonate with the spoken word and music. I wouldn't have such a love for writing if it weren't for Pac's lyrics. His art encouraged me that writing can be cool and can advocate for change. I wrote a lot, but never saw myself sharing it in spoken word or in a book. I never thought I would have an opportunity to be an author and share my love for writing without having a college degree or being hired by a newspaper. But many years since high school, God has blessed me with my dream career. God has given me opportunities to work side by side with doctors, professionals and accomplished authors in my research while writing my books. Don't ever let your past determine your future!

High School and Beyond

I graduated high school a year early and applied for university but was not able to afford the tuition payments. I then decided on a less expensive community college program. Working full time and attending college was a strain, so it took me nearly seven years to fully complete my associate's degree. After a year of struggling to afford basic necessities and attending college, I decided to enroll in the Army to help pay for college. My grandfather and Uncle had been in the Army and fought in WWII and Vietnam so thought I could follow in their footsteps. I thought this would be the best course in obtaining financial security, serving my country honorably and being able to someday complete college and then pursue a career in writing or journalism.

Army Life and my Assault

I joined the military and was so excited to serve my country and be a step closer to attending a four year university. I was excited to be able to go overseas and end the "war on terror" and kick some ass! What I experienced was something far from my ideas going into the military. These misconceptions filled my mind as I signed my life and body away to the government in one swoop of the pen.

I now see the military in a totally different light. The gaslighting of poor people under the assumptions of "fighting for freedom." I would quickly learn the fakeness of military life.

The way soldiers are treated, the lack of support and the toxic culture was eye opening to say the least.

I enlisted with the hope and vigor for a better life and a real chance to make something of myself. The whole time I was fighting for the false ideals of freedom. I found out that soldiers are expendable and not protected even in their own unit. Soon after I graduated basic training, I was violently raped and attacked by a fellow soldier. I was barely a new soldier and fresh into my service. I suffered a concussion from being thrown on the floor and hitting my head. I abruptly learned how the military treated its own, especially women. I returned late from the detail the night of my assault and even showed visible signs of an attack, bruising, bleeding and disorientation. I was not asked if I needed help. Instead I was put on restriction and the entire unit was also put on restriction to make an example of my coming in late. In typical Army fashion, when one soldier is reprimanded the whole squad or platoon can also be made to suffer consequences from one person. From this point on I was extremely ashamed and felt guilty for what happened and felt that somehow the attack was my fault. I took on the shame and embarrassment for the attack and had the entire company mad at me. The truth leaked out from my attacker of what happened but he spun the attack as somehow I wanted to be raped. This was a common ideal in Army life, the mistreatment of women and severe misogyny. I was continually berated with insults from all soldiers, male and female in my unit as a 'slut' or 'whore.'

I felt unsafe in the barracks and began to self-medicate with drugs, alcohol and excessive exercise. I began to believe the insults and thought I was a horrible human being. I had little to no support to turn to. The Army environment was very discriminating when it came to women. The environment was highly misogynistic. Talk of women being raped was common—every weekend to be exact but it was painted in a light of deep rooted misogyny where women are only good to be used for sex and they must have enjoyed being assaulted. If you see misogyny alive and well in America, just wait till you experience it 10-fold in the Army.

The intense trauma began to eat away at any self-worth I had remaining. I felt unsafe to come forward since the Army culture blamed women for rape. My brain became a cesspool of self-hate. Hate for others in charge. Hate for the authorities who were supposed to be looking out for all of us. Hate for the system for acting like this is ok and not providing justice. I hated the feeling of being all alone with a secret I could never tell because telling anyone could mean losing my job and credibility, so I tried to erase it from my memory.

My body and mind definitely did not forget about it. Though I would never speak of this incident, or my military career, for many, many years to come (avoidance), I would live in a traumatic pattern for years from the unresolved trauma. Onlookers would watch my life and see that something was wrong. I lived in fear and constantly seeking excitement and danger to fuel my need to feel alive and distract myself from my inner pain and shame.

I was discharged from the military for drinking when I was still in training. Before the discharge I tried to work with the commander and agreed to go to AA meetings to allow me to stay in the Army, but he did not honor our agreement and I was served discharge paperwork without an attorney or any support. I was sent with a one-way ticket to my hometown, left with undiagnosed PTSD, alcohol addiction and no money, housing, medical benefits or any form of assistance.

The Aftermath

The Army was my one and only plan, so this was devastating to me. Although I went to AA meetings, I was avoiding the true reason I turned to drinking as I thought I was worthless. It was hard to put down an addiction when the root cause was not addressed. It wasn't till many years later when in therapy I was able to release the guilt and shame from my attack and thus be also released from my need to drink.

The attack and the way I was let go by the Army was a life altering event. It engrained PTSD into my life and left me angry and a distrust for authority. Some people may crawl into a shell after rape and withdraw, while others, like me, might become more outgoing, seek adrenalin rush and toss respect for life aside. Your body remembers trauma. Our behaviors can show pain before you acknowledge it yourself.

PTSD Diagnosis

I ended up falling in love with a man who was also a Veteran. I had heard of combat PTSD, and saw how it affected him severely. I went one day to a local Vet Center seeking help for him or knowledge for myself on how to live with someone with PTSD. That day changed my life and not his, as I thought it might. Instead of the counselor wanting to talk about my boyfriend's PTSD, the counselor wanted us to talk about my military experience instead. I did not want to talk about it as I thought it was unimportant and it was highly embarrassing for me that I did not serve a full term or 'fight for freedom' or anything close to it. When I did finally talk about my service and what happened, the flood gates opened and I began to remember things I had pushed deep inside. Being in a safe environment and with a counselor trained in MST (Military Sexual Trauma) I was able to talk about my attack without judgment and in its true light, without misogynistic overtones. That day I was diagnosed with PTSD from the sexual assault in the military after a decade of living in undiagnosed PTSD hell. I went years just getting by, heavily drinking trying to avoid thinking about my trauma. I went years living in unnecessary guilt and shame for something that was done to me without my consent. I went years thinking I was a piece of shit for doing things that are only natural when you are hurting. The diagnosis I had wanted for my boyfriend ended up falling upon me. This was a complete eye-opener, as I had never heard you can have PTSD from things other than combat. I was so excited to have a glimmer of hope after being diagnosed and to have a name placed on what I was dealing with.

Healthcare and Moving Forward

My counselor helped me apply for VA healthcare and with her knowledge, expertise, kindness and support I am forever grateful. This access to healthcare changed my life. I was finally given the professional help I needed to deal with all the physical ailments related to the attack (like my TBI) and was able to access counseling.

Being awarded my benefits was an amazing, deeply healing moment. I did a lot of healing when I finally received the award letter in my hands. I received them by speaking up and breaking the silence over my attack. I felt like my recovery was just starting and I was learning to speak up for myself! This is when I began using all the resources available to me through the VA allowing me to try many therapies for PTSD.

I cannot speak enough about finding the right counselor. I advocate counseling in general, but finding a properly educated counselor that knows your specific situation and life experience is imperative. Not all counselors and doctors are alike. Some who are not trained in your specific trauma or background can end up causing you more harm than good.

Minorities face systematic and generational trauma in addition to their own everyday-life occurrences. If your therapist does not address or have knowledge about the systematic injustices and adversities you face as a minority, on top of the instances like rape or witnessing violence, then you will not be as well equipped to heal. I want to stress the importance of thoroughly vetting a counselor before you work with them. If they don't understand systematic trauma issues that you might be facing, (such as capitalism, racism and patriarchy, sexism, LGBTQ issues), your healing can be delayed when working with them and you could face more traumas as a result. It's going to have to be on you to ask the therapist's position and knowledge of your individual situation. It will be empowering to make sure you protect your best interest and self by fully vetting a therapist. Don't assume a therapist understands these issues. It is perfectly professional and acceptable to decline working with a therapist if they do not align to your values or hold a proper understanding on systematic oppression issues or your unique circumstances.

If it were not for my counselor's expertise and gentle guidance I would not be anywhere near where I am today. My counselor's help changed my life and this is why I advocate so strongly for everyone to never give up on counseling. I was not able to help my boyfriend as I had hoped, but I was able to help myself. This is truly the only thing we can do in life, is change ourselves and not others. (Which I also learned in counseling!)

Moving Forward with PTSD

As I began to dive into therapy and address my trauma I slowly felt better and freer to be me. I know that once I received the label of having PTSD, I knew how to go about seeking healing. I went on a mission to try every therapy for PTSD and all healing modalities available. I wanted to get past my trauma and start a new life. Living 10 years in unhappiness, I wanted nothing more than to be happy. I set down the shame and learned PTSD is a normal reaction to abnormal situations. I began to heal myself and was not afraid to try to overcome the past.

Going to therapy was a staple for me to talk and work through my trauma, but I also went further and experienced as many modalities that were available to me. Body work was monumental for me, but it had to be done on a consistent basis and I had to be completely comfortable with the person performing the massage or Reiki. This book outlines the therapies I explored in greater detail in other chapters. Once I got to a place of comfortability in my life I would try something new. I got to a place in life where I wanted to give back to other Survivors. This was therapy in itself and very healing. There is a natural progression to recovery and although you might not see progress on a daily basis, there will be progress in longevity.

Service Dog Gunner and the Nonprofit Formation

I decided to apply for a service dog (SD) through a local Veterans nonprofit when I had exhausted my other therapies. I had gained progress in my recovery, yet still needed help in public situations. After researching with my therapist and on my own, I decided to add a SD to my life. The local nonprofit accepted me into their program and I was very grateful. As a mother who was breastfeeding at the time I chose to use as little pharmaceutical help for my PTSD management as possible. A service dog seemed like a good alternative treatment. My love for dogs made this an easy choice. Luckily the addition of my Service Dog allowed me to regain my confidence and provided the support I needed to go out in public more comfortably.

My SD gave me a free feeling of independence leading me to want to share this same experience with other SA Survivors. Knowing there were civilians and veteran SA survivors out there who wanted service dogs but didn't have the resources for one was disheartening. In my mind, having a simple dog in a survivor's life could make a huge impact. With the help and advice from the founder of the Veteran's nonprofit that gave me Gunner, I was able to start a nonprofit of my own that directly assisted SA Survivors with PTSD. The need for a nonprofit that directly paired SD's with SA Survivors was and is still vital. Many nonprofits only assist combat PTSD Veterans or persons with physical disabilities who need service dogs. Starting Service Dog Strong is a mission I hope will continue to grow and raise awareness over SA-PTSD. The connection between SD's and SA Survivors cannot be overlooked. I have witnessed a transformation within myself and from other survivors who have gone through the program and their SD changed their life and trajectory with PTSD.

Once we launched SDS, the community support surrounding our mission was tremendous! It touched my heart and changed all the survivors who went through the program. We were so blessed to have such devoted supporters and volunteers keeping the program running and helping dogs and people! To be at this point in the journey was amazing to think about. I thank everyone who shared one of our posts or donated. SDS gave me the opportunity to meet the most amazing humans alive. The women who reached out to the nonprofit and joined the board were a blessing. Not only did these women work for free as volunteers, but they felt as strongly toward the SDS mission as I did. I couldn't believe how blessed and perfect everything fit into place and how God brought together the right people to start and keep this dream alive. Each donation to the nonprofit added up to helping dogs and people. Each donation touched my heart. I never really understood how hard it was for nonprofits to be sustained each year in order to provide help until I ran one myself. It truly is a business with deadlines and stress to stay out of the red just as a for-profit business. It was a large burden to raise donations because we always had an ongoing waitlist of survivors wanting to enter the program. Yet it was a beautiful sight to see when a survivor graduated with their dog and witness the change in their life.

Mom Life and a New Life Mission

Through my healing journey I was blessed with three incredibly beautiful, intelligent and uniquely different children. My children are the reason I keep going. When I first entertained the thought of becoming a mother, being a wholly healed person for my children sparked my drive to get treatment for my PTSD. My love for them and my attempts to make their lives better than mine was and is my driving force along with God's guidance and help.

I met my ex-husband before I was diagnosed with PTSD. We had met by creating what some would call a 'trauma bond.' I began my healing journey and soon became pregnant. Although you might strive for healing and to be the best person you can be, your partner, on the other hand, is a totally separate person whether you have children or not. They can be on different levels in their healing journey.

My accelerated healing created an imbalance in our relationship. My overall life view is much more positive and uplifting after dealing with my trauma instead of ignoring it and living in a victim mindset. I highlight this failed relationship to warn others that you will become a new version of yourself when you have done healing work. You will attract more like minded people and potentially have to leave some unhealed people in your life.

The more I worked through my trauma and learned healthy ways to live; the boundaries I set with my ex-husband became a problem. The healthier I became, the more I was able to identify abuse, that prior to my counseling, I would have somehow taken the blame or passed off as my partner just "having a bad day". I experienced his increasing need to control me and suffered intense intimate partner violence from him. I knew I had to leave the marriage as our children were witnessing his anger, violence and his alcohol addiction. The children began to model his abuse toward me and began calling me the same swear words their father addressed me as. This is an example of trauma causing more traumas.

Unfortunately, it is very common for women who are Survivors of SA to become victims of intimate partner violence. Abuse toward women and children is systematically normalized and allowed in our society. Survivors of SA and IPV are not readily believed and there are not enough resources or shelters available for women seeking safety from their abusers. Women and minorities suffer at the hands of the patriarchal system on a daily basis and it is time to recognize this and seek change.

Trauma is real. Systematic trauma is real. Healing and striving for health no matter what needs to be how you take care of yourself. Changing an entire system is something I cannot do alone, but changing myself is the one thing I can control. I want my children to see my strength and mirror this will to live a better life no matter what happens in your life. The continual blessings of God giving us another day is an opportunity to improve life through actions and resilience.

In divorcing my husband, I also had to step away from other obligations I once held deep love for. I had to step down from running the nonprofit. Stepping down was not my own idea, but the idea of the very board I had once voted for to volunteer for the nonprofit. As the divorce got messier and didn't show signs of ending (which is a natural occurrence when you leave an abuser; abuse rises when you try to leave), the nonprofit felt I needed to devote my time to the court case. The board voted me out of position during a zoom meeting. During this zoom I was also caring for my three children alone as a single mom. This was a day I will never forget, I was voting on staying the president of the nonprofit I founded, with the rest of the small board voting against me all while burning the kids chicken nuggets in the oven simultaneously.

Members of the board asked if they needed to call the fire department, but I insisted that I, more than anyone, can handle a small oven fire. I may not be the best cook but my cooking has taught me how to put out oven fires. The kids enjoyed eating out that night and getting pizza, so the burnt nuggets weren't a big deal! PTSD also has a way of allowing us to stay calm under large stressful situations. That was some zoom meeting to say the least. Moving forward after the board voted to have me step down until my divorce was finalized, I felt at peace with moving on. I did not want to stay somewhere that didn't see my value or could not support single mothers. I also had the desire to speak my mind, write books to help survivors on my own and not have to pass each social media post I made through a board meeting approval. PTSD has taught me to handle difficult situations in life. From small oven fires to being voted off of your own nonprofit board.

I knew although this turn of events could have devastated me, my recovery journey taught me to embrace change. My mission to promote service dogs with SA survivors and PTSD survivors will never change. My love and dedication to the mission cannot be voted out of me.

My healing journey has taught me that with each ending there is always a better beginning. This was a hard pill to swallow when I put my blood, sweat, tears and undying devotion into the mission of the nonprofit. I felt that my nonprofit work brought me balance in my life and gave me something to live for outside of my children. But I knew that when life hands you lemons, you must try and find a way to make lemonade or you can wallow in pain. I knew my worth and that no one can take away my advocacy and mission from me. I soon embraced the transition from working at the nonprofit and decided that it would be a better decision for me and my family to take the SA-PTSD and SD mission solo. No more zoom meetings while cooking for three hungry babies. Now I could promote my mission of PTSD recovery on my own time and terms and reach a greater worldwide audience. This was a much better fit as opposed to working within the confines of a small-state nonprofit. I decided to write books and speak on national stages and podcasts to advocate for all PTSD survivors. I could speak freely about all aspects of my life and journey without having a board filter my thoughts and ideas. Although I miss working directly with survivors and service dogs, my new mission has unlocked more opportunities than I could have ever imagined.

PTSD is such a large issue to address, but I feel called to raise awareness on not only SA-PTSD but gun violence PTSD as well, and this was something I could not do working for the nonprofit and working within the mission of providing SD's to SA survivors. God again, turned my pain into power. From the pain and heartbreak of having to leave the nonprofit and the people who worked with me side-by-side on the incredible mission and cared for deeply, God had other plans in store. I am glad I learned to embrace the change God had planned for me. If I were in the beginning of recovery I might have become severely depressed. But God created a more viable outlet for me to work with and allowed me to reach a much more diverse population and raise awareness for all forms of PTSD and I'm so glad I embraced it. I needed a career where I could work on my own time schedule and around my children's timing as well.

My PTSD and the Future

PTSD recovery has taught me so many coping skills. PTSD and sharing my story has brought me to meet so many amazing people. PTSD has brought me misery and severely impacted my relationships and brought me to meet and bond with sick people. PTSD has forced me to need a SD. PTSD has brought my wonderful SD into my life that I wouldn't change for the world. PTSD has caused me to lose jobs and my PTSD has created an outlet for me to create my own job and hire myself to become an author and speaker. Take time to heal from

PTSD and life can bloom into something more beautiful than your plan for your life could have ever been.

List of Steps for healing from PTSD

1. **<u>Get the Drugs out the way</u>**

   Detoxifying. Healing from PTSD will not happen if you are numbing yourself with substances.

2. **<u>Finding financial freedom to afford time to heal</u>**

   Healing takes time. There are inpatient centers for recovery that can accelerate your journey when you can focus on yourself for weeks at a time without distractions. Having the finances in order to take the time to work through PTSD is essential for faster healing. Being financially free to do this can come with its own challenges,but seeking outside help is going to be something you should highly consider. A few weeks completely devoted to you can equal years of relief.

3. **<u>Self love</u>**

   Finding a reason to fight through your trauma is imperative. Loving yourself enough to take the time to do the hard work is going to be essential. Loving the people in your life is also a good reason. Being fed up with your circumstances, desiring to have a better future for yourself and those around you is a good start to finding peace and healing in your life.

4. **Forgiveness for self and others**

   Finding peace with PTSD is going to involve self reflection and a willingness to let go of what you cannot control. This is summed up as having forgiveness for yourself and for others.

5. **Different therapies to try**

   Willingness to try everything possible until you find what works for a healthy lifestyle will be important. Each trauma can affect people differently so finding the right healing modality is important. Keep in mind that most people find relief by using multiple modalities.

6. **Exercise and diet**

   Healthy eating habits can help to accelerate a healthy mental state of mind.

7. **Transcendental meditation**

   Chanting meditations has been found to be effective for people with PTSD. It is an easy way to calm the mind and takes little effort and focus to participate in this form of meditation. Meditation has been proven to reduce PTSD symptoms when practiced regularly.

8. **Healthy hobbies**

   Healthy hobbies need to be added to your new 'PTSD free' lifestyle. To achieve different outcomes in life, you have to DO things differently. Adding new rhythms and new positive activities will accelerate relief from negative feelings. For example: exchange Friday night at the bar with Friday night at the gym or going for a walk with friends.

9. **Helping others/community involvement/mentoring/ volunteering**

This step should not be overlooked. Stepping outside your PTSD shell is essential by giving back to others. It can bring new insight and gratitude into your life as well as show you that at any stage of your journey you are needed in this world. Helping others can bring peace.

CHAPTER 4

Financial Freedom

Recovery can be sped up or hindered by certain external and internal factors. Finances are one of them. I would not be doing justice to my fellow survivors if I ignored this important external factor. Just as many of us have experienced systematic inflicted traumas based on our gender or race, trauma of not having financial resources is another. If we do not have access to proper medical care or the ability to take time from work to heal or check into a detox or recovery center, recovery will not happen as fast. Capitalism puts a price on our health and mental well being. As much as this is unfair and unjust, I want to reiterate the need for the survivor to keep their determination strong when trying to obtain proper medical care for a time to heal.

Healing from trauma not only takes time, but it takes money. I lived 10 years without health care which greatly hindered me from getting the mental and physical help I needed. If you are struggling to provide yourself with food and shelter, your emotional needs will not be on the top of your list of necessities. This is explained in Maslow's hierarchy of needs. If you don't have health care, or you cannot afford the time to manage your health, you will not progress physically or mentally. Overcoming PTSD means you will have to put your health as your top priority. Financial resources and health care will have to be prioritized in order to be able to have access to certain PTSD treatments.

It is necessary to take a break and focus on healing. Seeking out social services, health care, nonprofits or churches that might help with medical, food or housing costs is going to be essential in helping you reach your goal of lowering your PTSD symptoms. For Veterans and their families, there are free Vet Centers throughout the US that offer counseling. Most other programs offer sliding scales for services based on income.

The VA's PTSD clinics or civilian clinics can require lengthy in-patient stays. If you cannot afford to take off work to go to counseling or doctor's appointments, it is obvious your healing will be delayed. I encourage you to make yourself the top priority because when you are able to handle your symptoms better, your entire life will be uplifted. If you are looking for a reason not to make progress, or say it's too hard, then your financial situation could potentially hold you back. Please exhaust any free resources online and in your community.

Financial freedom equals opportunities and greater access to healthcare in America and around the globe. Healthcare is all but a luxury, I am very sad to say. I do believe this is why a lot of persons with PTSD do not seek the help they need. I do not have an answer on how to make healthcare affordable to all, but I can only encourage you to not give up when you are seeking the healthcare help you need. Health is wealth and wealth can equal health when you can afford the time to heal. I encourage you to seek out help for low-income health care options online and seek out free counseling resources online or at your local health department, shelter or library. Many PTSD clinics and therapy offices offer sliding scales for persons without health insurance, you just have to ask. There are not always enough resources available, this is why we must take self-healing into our own hands. Health is true wealth.

Key Points:

Finances have to be addressed in order to make time and space for self healing work

Social services can be utilized

Clearing your schedule by taking time off from work or responsibilities will pay off when you devote time to your healing.

Determine how much time off you are able to take in order to devote to yourself while not defaulting too far behind on bills and adding to your stress

Reach out to community resources if possible

CHAPTER 5

AA/NA Get the Drugs Out of the Way

This chapter encourages sobriety in order to handle the underlying emotional issues caused by PTSD. I found quicker recovery once I put in the hard work to detox first. It is counterproductive to use substances that numb emotional memories and distract you from reality while trying to get to the bottom of self healing work.

It is important to remove toxic substances from the body when trying to get your PTSD symptoms under control. Drugs and alcohol can be contributing to the imbalance of emotions and their ups and downs. I do not mean medications prescribed to you by a doctor, but substances that are not prescribed can lead to addiction problems and cause depression. Self-medicating can leave you numb thereby avoiding real emotions and the underlying reasons behind your trauma. Addictive substances can add to your trauma. Once the drugs, alcohol, and the masking of pain is cleared away, you are better able to attack the underlying cause of why you began to use in the first place. You will have to be vulnerable. Healing from PTSD means getting rid of the pain and trauma that's bothering you and preventing you from moving forward.

When there is nothing to numb your emotions, the mask will come off and you will be left with your "gasp" emotions. Yes, emotions are good, bad and ugly. PTSD recovery will involve doing many hard things, but I believe you have already made it through the hardest part of understanding your emotions and avoidance behaviors. The trauma that comes afterward is secondary. This healing process is about becoming free. Anything getting in your way of moving forward and keeping you in an addicted mindset of daily torment needs to go.

PTSD symptoms will be easier to manage once your dependencies are under control or completely eliminated. Being addicted to something is not easy. It can be extremely hard for some to be ready to face a new life without their daily addiction. Addictions can be the solution to many for handling pain and PTSD. It is a harmful solution and will cause more harm to you in the end than relief. Please consult your doctor and care team when you have an addiction to properly and safely find the best recovery plan that is right for you.

How I became sober was with the help of the 12 Steps. They are used as the backbone of AA/NA programs and are used in other recovery programs as well. The general steps are often copied and used in similar programs. I advocate that you find what works for you. If the 12 Steps don't work for you and you have genuinely tried them, then please try something else until you can be substance free. For me, the steps were effective and genuinely life changing. The 12 Steps are simple, yet not easy to accomplish. The steps are there to help you deal with your entire trauma and to clear away the substances. You will have to be very brave to achieve sobriety, but it is a journey worth the struggle.

I know from being addicted that substances are used as a solution to your trauma. Drugs and alcohol are a way to forget or numb your thoughts. When you take away the substances you are left with no way to cope and deal with life. Recovery programs are developed for that purpose. Just taking away your unhealthy solution is not going to automatically solve your problems. It can often make things harder for you and this is why you must have a strong mental mindset that sobriety is your goal. You must be prepared to substitute your unhealthy addictions for healthier ones and be active in addressing your emotions and trauma so that you don't slide back into those substances when things go wrong.

Recovery can bring such beautiful things into your life. You will never get to experience life to the fullest when you are reliant on a substance every day. Obviously seeing recovery in action is very attractive. Doing it is extremely difficult and will take every ounce of strength, determination and surrender to a new lifestyle. Sobriety can be an unknown lifestyle for you at first, which can be scary. But waking up without the need to get high is a much better, freeing feeling than drugs will ever be. Living life on life's terms can be freeing and you never know what you have missed until you give sobriety a chance.

Sobriety has to be truly wanted. Some will lose everything and still not surrender to sobriety. We all know people who have lost their battle with addiction. You don't need me to scare you into trying sobriety. If you truly want to overcome PTSD symptoms, then removing substances from your life will greatly improve your chances of success.

I have to acknowledge the great power of my addictions and the even greater power of the Great Magnet who kept me alive. God gave me a second chance at life, and I will be forever grateful. God has watched over me and I do not take His protection for granted.

Devoting some time in therapy and a recovery program could leave someone addiction free. I believe there is always hope for everyone, but you must want it more than being comfortable in your pain. Your whole life can be ruined by something that happened in the past if you don't fight for your recovery and a new future.

I believe addiction needs to be looked at differently in our society. I have a dear friend that everyone that knows him, knows he 'loves' to drink. He never told anyone of his childhood trauma. I see that he does not 'love' to drink but he attempts daily to mask his childhood trauma. The world saw an alcoholic, I saw a hurt individual. He doesn't love his addiction and the aftermath it creates. Yet, until the trauma is addressed, masking and addiction is inevitable. There is a saying, "You may have another drunk or drink in you, but you may not have another sobriety in you." I think it goes both ways. Sobriety is hard to achieve and can take a while to enjoy, but living with addiction is also hard. Who really knows when that drink or drug will be your last?

I don't need to go into all my horror stories and nightmares and close calls alcohol and drugs have caused me. When you are dealing with pain all the drugs and alcohol in the world will not be enough to mask the pain. Drinking and drugging does not erase it. It will only add to your issues. The underlying cause of the pain and trauma is still there. Using it does not get rid of it. If you are using it to mask these internal painful emotions and memories, then you will have to use it daily. More and more your tolerance to the drug increases while the pain continues to grow as your body and mind trigger you more and more to deal with this hurt. You can keep ignoring it, but it will never go away. It will only increase. Then the use will cause you greater pain. Maybe you lose your job, your family or become ill. Don't let the trauma keep controlling you! It's your time to control the new life that's ahead.

My personal recovery story.

I wanted to live the Army life and do my best. But the mental anguish and constant reminder and fear of seeing my attacker after being raped in the Army prevented that. I had no idea how to cope with the distress or who I could feel safe talking to about it all. The drink quickly became the only escape dealing with my symptoms. I found some kind of support and acceptance with other alcoholics. The lack of safety in the Army led me to totally lose hope in life. Drinking was the solution. I had no interest in quitting the drug that numbed the pain. I look back and wonder what would have happened if I were asked, "How are you doing?" or "Is there anything you want to talk about that is bothering you?"

The only help the Army had to offer was an AA group at the base a few times a week. I was the youngest one at these meetings. I was 20 years old. I was thinking I was just an alcoholic and my trauma was not valid. I thought the booze was the real problem and I didn't understand why I just couldn't quit. Why would I want to be sober and relive the thoughts of the attack over and over again? I had to maintain a constant avoidance of my feelings, especially having to see my abuser on a daily basis. Seeing him excel in the Army, seeing him promoted and me being restricted was heartbreaking.

Drugs and alcohol can be the mask covering the true problems. Addiction is horrible because it can become your whole life. However, the drugs are not the problem. Trauma is the main cause of addiction. Making drugs illegal is not the solution either. The system is not there to rehabilitate people with emotional problems that lead them to use in the first place. Making drugs illegal and putting those who are in poverty and sell these illegal substances in jail does not solve the poverty or addiction problem. Once a person has a record, who is at fault? The dealer for selling something to people who willingly want to buy their product? Or the buyer for wanting such harmful substances? Are they really entrepreneurs? Having been on both sides of the coin I believe that healing and recovery should be the focus in our society. Locking poverty stricken individuals away again and again for victimless crimes is not the solution. Nor is shaming someone who has experienced trauma and is led to seeking the cheapest form of healthcare that is available.

AA meetings on the Army base proved to be a wonderful introduction to healing. Until I had the realization in therapy, almost a decade later, that I was drinking and drugging because of my rape, I couldn't fully understand how to put down the booze and drugs. I had to heal my emotional trauma before I could give up drinking. My head was full of pain and trauma and my body was full of toxins. I had no resources and many distraught memories I wanted to forget. I was only left with my alcohol addiction by my side. It was my only "friend." It gave me a false sense of happiness. All the support I didn't have I found through alcohol and drugs. My use of drugs would get worse. Drugs became an easier, longer and stronger way to mask the ugly thoughts and feelings. It was a "more bang for your buck" type of deal, with no added smell on your breath.

My strong deep down desire for healing also drove me to keep this vision of a better life for myself in view. It was fueled by my disgust of how I felt each day and how my life went nowhere the more I used. This strong desire to make life better was the start of the healing path that would eventually lead me to start *Service Dogs Strong*. Whatever you are facing in life, don't give up! Never give up and never leave your dream of a better life behind no matter how bad things get or may seem. If given another day, then you can rebuild your life. I know this to be true. It will take a while for—your drive and your actual life—to coincide. But keep that dream alive. Change starts with an intention. Positive thinking and thoughts envisioning a better life are the gateway to making them happen. Positive thoughts backed by positive action is the key to true success.

I had remembered the AA meetings on base. I remembered how welcoming the members were and how much I loved the positiveness and understanding of the group. Just like finding the right counselor, finding the right sponsor that works for you is important. I was told that the easiest way to make AA work is to get through all the steps as quickly as possible. Yes, go through them completely and thoroughly, but fast. If you are drinking or drugging to the point you could potentially die any day from your use, you need to get through the 12 Steps as soon as possible to save your life. It's 12 Steps for a reason. Just doing 6 or 11 won't work. This was crucial for me. I could not skip steps or skip having a sponsor. I did have a sponsor for a time who wanted to take a whole year to complete all 12 steps. This was out of context and who wants to wait a whole year to get sober? I didn't want to wait a whole year to feel better and beat my addiction. Who knew if I had a year left in me? I threw myself wholeheartedly into healing and working the steps as fast as possible. I found a new sponsor and completed the steps in 3 months.

Your recovery depends on finding the right sponsor or support, who will work the steps with you and give you in a timely pace. The sponsor works for you, so please choose wisely and don't feel obligated to stay with someone who is not working with you. It is more about the steps than the sponsor, but make sure the sponsor knows how to take you through them so you can achieve sobriety as soon as possible. If the AA program isn't your choice for recovery that is not a problem. There are many other programs that can help like SMART Recovery or Harm Reduction Therapy, please search for alternatives and find what you're comfortable with.

AA is not regulated and there can be predators in the program or those who do not practice the steps correctly. Please be aware that even in recovery people can try and take advantage of you at your lowest point. The program is volunteer lead so please this might not be the best fit for everyone. There are other sobriety programs available one can try, although not all are free. For me, the 12 steps were very foundational in helping me to create a healthier life. I have heard for others it has not been as helpful for them and there can be very dangerous people in these meetings as not everyone is fully recovered. So please be aware and vigil. These same 12 Steps are often used in many recovery settings even outside of the typical AA meetings. Abstinence based recovery has been proven to be effective in breaking any addiction. Finding whatever works to keep you sober is the goal and there are many programs available regulated, or volunteer.

Never give up on your sobriety. I have relapsed many times but always felt better about my life when sober. I keep trying and I hope you do too. If anything, give it a try for a time. It can take one day at a time, or one hour, or even a minute at a time. Sobriety does get easier, but you will always need to be proactive. You will always have to be vigilant and practice the steps daily in your life to stay sober. Sobriety can be a new adventure and a true gift.

I wish everyone who is in the struggle peace and strength to overcome and live the good life on life's terms.

"God grant me the serenity to accept the things I cannot change, courage to change the things I can, and the wisdom to know the difference."

Key Points:

Recovery can go hand-in-hand with drug and alcohol detoxification

Relying on substances to adapt to PTSD will prolong the process.

Getting the substances out of your life will lead to more room for actual healing modalities and allow you to have a clear mind.

CHAPTER 6

Self-Love Chapter

Loving yourself enough to want better for your life is true recovery! Finding love for who you are for no other reason than just because you are you is imperative. Love yourself despite your condition and experiences. Recovery will require you to love yourself stronger than your old habits to self destruct. Loving yourself and taking care of yourself will create space for you to show up for those you love and care about.

I devoted a single chapter to self-love because it holds so much importance. Self-love is a huge accomplishment. The messier life has been, it can be hard to view yourself as deserving of love from yourself. Self-love is not selfish! Taking time for ourselves is not selfish. Taking adequate time to heal, detoxify or visit a recovery center is an essential foundation in self-love. Love for yourself will grow when you continue to make positive choices in your life and honor your body. Even with the hard circumstances you had to endure, you deserve love from self and others. Love for yourself should be unconditional. The more you give yourself grace and love yourself, the more recovery will grow.

Survivors and PTSD victims can find self-love a hard concept to practice due to the trauma making us feel inadequate or damaged. We could feel shame for things we had to do to survive. We tend to put the needs of others before our own. We keep those around us happy to avoid conflict, thus allowing our boundaries to be crossed and hurting ourselves more in the process. This is not loving ourselves when we avoid bringing up our own needs or feelings for the sake of avoiding conflict. Self love will involve learning to speak up for your needs because you love yourself. Self love is showing yourself grace and understanding you did the best you could in the moment.

As you further your healing journey, please change your thinking around your self-worth. As you learn healthier ways to deal with trauma, know that you are going to have to reshape the way you see yourself as well. A healthy view of self is to see yourself as invaluable and worthy of love and respect, even if you have not experienced this before. When you have been abused, you might not have a proper loving view of yourself, or know what love looks like. This is a journey that can grow with the aid of a counselor. Love is a free feeling. The more in tune you are with your body, you will be able to feel a person's intentions and feel if you are being loving and kind to yourself.

Setting Boundaries is Self Love

Practice self-love by starting to do something nice for yourself. Taking care of your outer appearance can be a good start and also can positively change how others treat you. Showing the world you have self esteem and good hygiene creates an atmosphere of self love. Self love can mean actions, material things or just saying 'no' to things that stretch you thin and do not align with your goals and values. Then saying 'yes' to the things that do. If you come from a traumatic childhood, you can carry low self-worth. As an adult it is time to reevaluate. Do you want to keep dressing down to the level you feel about yourself, or try a new habit of dressing up? This small habit of proper grooming and buying a few outfits that make you look your best can really change a person's outlook (and the world's outlook) about who you are.

Overcoming Negative Self Perception is Self Love

When living with and through unhealthy behaviors and unhealthy toxic people around you, naturally you can expect bad behavior and the thoughts that you must be worthless if this is how others treat you. You can become conditioned to take the abuse and be tricked into thinking this is the best life can offer. Upbringing can affect this thinking. Children who grow up in traumatic households have no choice but to live and grow in that unhealthy environment. They can't escape when their boundaries are continually being crossed.

Their emotions are being disrespected and unattended. This treatment becomes ingrained into their whole being. As an adult you must purposefully relearn what self-love is.

Survivors can learn self-love even when it feels uncomfortable. When setting your boundaries and teaching others how you expect to be treated, it can feel 'fake' or that you are being harsh. Often it involves merely removing yourself from a situation or person who chooses to continue to show you disrespect. You're not that stuck child anymore. You do have options as to how you will be treated and whom you will spend your time with.

I had to imagine what it would look like to love myself. How would I take time in the day to set certain boundaries in order to take care of myself? I had to imagine what a healthy relationship would look like and imagine how I really wanted to be treated by others. I had to do some really hard self-evaluation. What did I stand for and what kind of life did I want? Did I want to continue living a fake life where I would smile and say "ok" to everything and everyone, while on the inside being angry because I really wanted to speak and say what was on my mind? I had to learn to love myself and believe I was worth something to be able to speak up and say "NO."

Saying "No" was a huge task for me and I believe it is for any survivor. It can seem like a hard thing to do at first. 'No' is a complete sentence. Saying 'No' should be a sign of self-love and respect. Trust that if someone doesn't value you, they will ignore or pressure your 'No' until you give in to their demands.

I had made it out of the Army alive after my assault. I lived through addiction and homelessness and that didn't take me out. Now I wanted to live the best life possible. I had to truly believe that I was worthy of love and respect no matter what I had been through. I had to search out positive ideas and images on what this even looked like. I knew there was a better way to live and wanted to search for this until I found it. I kept vigilantly striving to be able to show my children a better way to live.

It all starts with self-love. You can do something for yourself right away. Showers, a walk, a night away, meditation, or break up with someone who crosses your boundaries. Write a list of what your boundaries are. Clean up your space, put some make-up on your face or take some off, give yourself a massage . . . it can be so many different things. If it makes you feel good and helps to make you smile and brings you peace, that's self-love.

Loving yourself when Parenting

PTSD parents need to take their self-care to a higher level since they have to care for their children along with themselves, so this means twice the risk for burnout. Being super vigilant around practicing self care and self love will mean you are able to be the best parent for your children. Taking care of yourself and your needs means you will be available for your children in a healthier way. Loving yourself is loving your children too. Taking your time for yourself to maintain your emotions and needs will set you up to handle the hard situations that arise when parenting. When your children see you modeling self-love, this act will carry over into their own lives. Taking a meditation break is a better example than being burnt out and portraying to your children that parents are somehow super-human robots that never need rest.

Treat self-care like your survival. Going without self-care breaks as parents can be toxic and unsustainable. Even as a single parent you must find a way to schedule a break. Scheduling more vacations (or stay-cations), visiting parks can be a good way to find breaks within your budget. You can set time during the day when you go to your room to meditate for 20 minutes, and the children in theirs or setting them up with a quiet activity, can be beneficial to the family as a whole. Once you establish that you will need a few minutes to regroup and meditate, you can invite your children to meditate with you. Having PTSD requires a lot from you and so does being a parent. The only solution to finding health and better management for these symptoms is to take more deep breathing breaks, meditation breaks and find gentle ways to reduce your stress multiple times during the day.

When a parent has elevated symptoms of PTSD, having children can raise their stress. The family has already experienced many moments of tension. PTSD moments, if not counteracted, can create an unhealthy environment for all members of the family, not just the person with PTSD. For any parent (PTSD sufferer or not), parenting will test your limits and exhaust you. This is why the deliberate need for the PTSD parent to find multiple times a day to take a break, no matter how short, is essential. Being in tune with your body will be important so you can know when you need a break. You're not only doing it for your own health, but for the family. My children were my motivation to become the healthiest Mom I could be. The motivation to show my kids happiness and health over adversity pushed me to find PTSD solutions that worked.

PTSD families need to treat fun times and breaks as a top priority. Create as many positive experiences as possible to counteract the PTSD symptoms and the potentially uncomfortable situations the family has been in before you sought help for your symptoms. Keep in mind that for a person with PTSD, scheduled fun times can also add to a person's stress. I recall many vacations that were set with good intentions, turned into nightmares because my husband's PTSD stress from being in public was too much for him. We all suffered from his inability to regulate himself. So, plan accordingly with breaks and proper limits on what is realistic. Try outings alone at first, then bring the family with you if being in public is a big trigger for you. You are responsible for taking care of yourself so that you can be there for your family and enjoy outings in the future.

Traditional vacations can be very expensive. I am not advocating going into debt for a needed break; this would be counterproductive and would only create more stress. Also, for some with PTSD the traditional vacation might even be a trigger. Looking for parks, beaches, hikes and nature stay-cations with less people can be a safe way to go for a break. Whatever it may look like for you to escape for some moments of rest, find a way to make it happen. Just keep in mind 'MORE BREAKS' to help calm your nervous system as it can be hyperextended with PTSD.

Reaching out to others for help to allow you to take breaks is also self-love. You may have to ask others for childcare help so that you can take care of yourself. Being able to vocalize your needs and ask for help unapologetically is essential. I believe it shows strength, not weakness.

PTSD survivors will require more breaks to avoid an overflow of the freeze/fawn/flight/fight nervous system. Breaks give you time for yourself, help to create new positive pathways in your brain, and can even become a positive to your PTSD. Adding positive experiences to my week made a huge difference to me. It was better than staying at home thinking about my situation and being mad about it. Do something to make your life better. You are going to have to reach down deep, find a little self-love to entertain a change in life. Life isn't going to change for you.

Deciding to re-enter social media to make a plea for help and support to start *Service Dogs Strong* was a big enough push for me to decide to put my story out there. What a beautiful surprise it was! The kindness from strangers was the reassurance I needed to put my faith back into humanity. The kindness from the community brought SDS to life from just a dream. Was it hard to share my story? Yes. Was it scary? Yes. Was it uncomfortable, self-doubting? Yes. Was it necessary and worth it? Yes! Taking positive chances can be amazing! I had to be very far into my healing and recovery to feel safe enough to take such chances. I did go over my story and experiences many times through exposure and talk therapy. By the time I began to appear on the public platform, I was comfortable telling my story. This didn't happen overnight.

It all comes down to self-love. Love yourself enough to want a different life. Love yourself enough to change when it's hard and uncomfortable. Sometimes it just takes being fed-up with where you're at to take chances. Self-love is something that is easy to talk about but hard to do. Self-love has to be earned and learned by practicing it over and over.

Staying optimistic was a mindset change I had to take on in order to get to the next level. Imagine things going right-self-love. Show yourself some grace when you make mistakes. Love needs to start from within by making healthy changes in your life. You will love yourself more when your positive changes add up and start to take effect in your life. Your accomplishments will trigger you to be proud of yourself and love yourself more. The more you love yourself, the more love you will have to give to others. The more love you show others, the more love you will get in return.

Key Points

Learning to love yourself is an important concept to embody when trying to rebuild your life

Self love is key to starting your healing journey and the reason you are compelled to complete it.

Self love will require greater effort into positive experiences than the pull to return to self-destructive behavior

Healing goes hand-in-hand with self love

Loving yourself as a parent shows you love your children.

CHAPTER 7

Forgiveness

Healing comes with self reflection and the reflection from those who have affected our lives. Forgiveness is not an easy choice. Anger can linger and grow if you hold onto the hurt brought on from not forgiving. There is a saying that forgiveness is for you and not for the people who harmed you. This was very true for me. I decided to release the people who caused me harm by forgiving them. I did it for me and not to absolve them from wrongdoing or to say that everything is 'ok.' I forgave in order to bring myself peace and to elevate to a higher energy than the pain that was brought into my life.

Forgiveness is probably one of the hardest steps in recovery. My hate and anger were fueled by the person who violated me, the people who did nothing to protect me, the authorities that did not do their job but hindered justice, and all the people who did not support me in my difficulties. I have lived with individuals who had PTSD from many different traumatic events: loss of a parent, combat, inner city violence (witnessing, being involved and a victim), sexual assault and molestation. Though all these situations were different, the reactions and coping mechanisms were similar.

There is no excuse for how I was treated, but never-the-less, my un-forgiveness was starting to hurt me. Not forgiving was a punishment I was inflicting upon myself. Hanging onto the anger, pain and having to constantly think of my abuser over and over again was hurting me when the trauma was supposed to be over.

Generally speaking, forgiving someone can lead you to peace sooner. It can propel your self-healing and your journey. It is hard to do. To release hate will bring you to another level. It can take a long time to get to a place where you can feel ready to forgive. I don't think forgiveness is essential to healing but it can be another step toward finding your peace.

Holding onto resentment will eventually lead you to relapse and possibly treat others in a non-peaceful way. It is said that forgiveness does not mean you are giving the person a "get out of jail free card," but instead you are releasing yourself from the internal jail you have put yourself in. Your jail is having memories come up again and again. In the process, you are stirring up more anger and resentment. The internal prison of the mind can be a place where you would want your perpetrators to feel as you did and wishing ill-will upon them. This creates more anger, hate and negativity within yourself and distracts you from your healing purpose and peace.

My attacker was promoted in the Army, while I got my discharge papers. Peace and forgiveness must come from acceptance of the situation and knowing you are unable to ever change it. For you to have a better life, you must fight your inner will that wants to continue the anger. Instead, find forgiveness within yourself, FOR yourself. It has nothing to do with the other people involved. It does not mean you are saying the situation was just or right, but you do have to find a way to let that person go completely from your life and thoughts.

If you do not forgive, hate and anger will control your life. This will give the person (or unjust situation) more power over you and it will continue to control you! It may seem at first that anger and hate is so very hard to just 'let go of.' However, I want to say that negative people and circumstances will keep haunting you and controlling your life if you don't continually work on forgiveness of the person and situation. Do not give them anymore control over your life!

Forgiveness does not mean what they did was ok. Forgiveness is just for you! It takes almost superhuman, Jesus-like strength to do this. Luke 23:34 states, *"Father, forgive them for they know not what they are doing."* Most likely, the person might not even feel bad for what they did. For people to commit such acts they most likely did not have any moral compass to begin with or they hold deep seeded trauma which prevents them from feeling. Holding on to a hope where you might one day see justice or receive an apology from these people is only going to delay your best life. You might be holding onto the hate or vision of justice forever.

I found a helpful exercise in counseling that helped get the process of forgiveness going. Imagine what forgiveness looks and feels like just to "trick" you into actually doing it. Imagine sitting down with the person and saying or writing down how you feel. You don't need the person to actually be there. It is just an exercise. If you are not able to forgive just yet, imagine the person saying 'sorry, ' or whatever you need them to do or say, so you can feel the release of anger. In many circumstances it is inadvisable or impossible to confront your abuser. This exercise can help with initiating forgiveness.

I used my anger to fervently work and press for change in my life and in the world. It was the deciding factor that motivated me to publicly tell my story. Wholeheartedly, unforgiveness is far more detrimental to you and your livelihood than it is good. Don't hold onto hate in your heart for those people who don't even deserve another thought in your life. Don't degrade yourself to their level of human existence. If someone has crossed you, they will have to deal with their life— their dreams, their actions, their wrong-doing. Don't make yourself suffer more by holding onto hate and plotting vengeance, or just more negativity in your mind taking up space and energy that could be used for good and self-improvement. The best 'pay back' for anyone who has hurt you is living your life as if they never existed. This can only be achieved by your self-healing progress and finding forgiveness in your heart so you can truly move on from your past. I pray you will ask for help, if needed, to be able to come to the point where you can forgive others and even forgive yourself.

Key Points:

Forgiveness for yourself and others can lighten your emotional load and accelerate healing, although forgiveness of others is a choice and not necessary to find healing.

CHAPTER 8

Importance of Exercise, Healthy Living and Eating

This chapter will outline what I found helpful in my healing journey. Your physical health is directly connected to your mental health, and vice versa. If you are having a difficult time with PTSD, give yourself a boost and get some exercise. Your eating habits and physical routine are very important to the way your mind operates. Mental, physical and spiritual health is all interconnected.

The longer I lived with verbal abuse, isolation and the lack of respect in my marriage, the more my body began to catch up with that depressed lifestyle. I suffered from low energy which led to my being overweight. My skin was always a mess and my hair didn't grow. When you're living in an unsafe household the constant emotional abuse of 'fight/flight/freeze/

fawn' mentality, your brain becomes damaged. It is harder to articulate your thoughts, and your body slowly deteriorates. You gradually become mentally unstable because your brain is constantly being subjected to life-or-death conditions and never given time to heal.

How is it possible for your brain and body to relax if you are living 24/7 with an abuser? How can you recover from PTSD if you are not giving your body what it needs, such as good nutrition, physical exercise and rest? When your body believes it is in a life-or-death situation 24/7, recovering from PTSD is going to take intense counseling and help.

If we don't get enough good rest, our body is unable to heal itself. When we are sleeping, our body goes into a 'rest, digest and restore' mode. Our body heals best when asleep. It can focus solely on healing and doesn't have to give energy to bigger tasks like eating, walking and staying alert for survival. Our body can take its time to heal when asleep. That is why sleep is so important. If you have children, the best advice is to take the time to sleep when they do. House chores can wait. Your health is much more important than having a spotless house, especially when we have PTSD going on. Sleep and rest is vital!

There is a mind, body and soul connection. It is very important to maintain a healthy body as well as maintain your mental health. Below is an article that outlines the connection between poor mental health and the adverse effects it can have on your body. I would like to emphasize that the article states, "Healing is possible." This article will explain the effects of abuse on the body and demonstrate the mind and body connection, as emotions can affect us physically.

https://psychcentral.com/health/effects-of-emotional-abuse

PTSD is 'emotional,' yet can have severe physical implementations. Making sure you physically take care of your body is extremely important when you have PTSD.

Finding the right exercise and healthy eating habits helped greatly in my PTSD recovery. Staying physically and mentally fit requires dedication on all levels. Since our whole health is about being mentally, physically and spiritually healthy, I spent just as many hours in the gym as I did in a therapy chair. We are only able to achieve true total health when the wheels of our mind, body and spirit are all turning together unblocked and open. Western medicine doesn't acknowledge anything other than the physical body, but if you study eastern medicine, it teaches about chakras and meridian lines that connect the spiritual body with the physical.

Consult your doctor before changing your diet or physical activity routine.

Physical activity releases natural endorphins throughout your body making it more difficult to feel depressed when working out. Healthy nutrition is going to provide you with the energy you need to work out. At times of emotional distress, I found it almost impossible to stick to my health routine and diet of choice. When depressed I found my body craving comfort foods and quick energy like sugar and carbohydrates. My body was screaming out for help to counteract the depression and low energy. This can become a vicious cycle. The longer you subject your body to toxins and refined sugar, the more your body will crave it. Detoxing from this addiction can be long and hard.

Sugar and processed foods are like a drug. Ingesting sugar will make you want it more, and the more you consume, the more you are unfulfilled. You can become addicted to sugar and processed foods because your taste buds become accustomed to fake foods, fake flavors. It's a quick sugar rush. The more sugar you ingest, the worse your body will feel because these fake foods are not nourishing and highly addictive. The true natural foods from God will be a long lasting, healthy investment for your body. The body is designed to heal itself and get rid of toxins before they multiply into cancers and other ailments. The continual daily stress on our bodies from environmental pollution, the chemicals on our clothes, the man-made chemicals we have all around us in cleaners, perfumes and products we put on our skin, make it difficult to stay well.

The more active you are, the more you must eat. Finding balance between eating healthy and physical exercise is crucial for any lifestyle, especially in trying to combat PTSD symptoms. Any positive addition to your physical health increases brain function and helps to alleviate depression. Exercising has helped my mood and positive outlook. My journey into yoga helped me learn the right things to eat. Diet and exercise proved to be a huge victory moment in my life.

Not counting calories, eating natural foods and just knowing my body worked best for me. Eating when hungry and learning the signs of your body that tell you when to stop eating are also important. PTSD made me disconnected with my body at times and I would forget to eat. Being in tune with your body will make you in tune to your mind. Keep your foods organic to avoid harmful pesticides and chemicals. Self-love and commitment will help you stick to a healthy diet. It takes four weeks to create a habit, so don't give up!

Making goals small and obtainable is better than setting goals too high and feeling bad about yourself when you are not able to devote enough time to them. When in recovery and learning new patterns it's important to take small steps. The health of your body should be a priority for you to live your best life and to feel well. Our emotions will be more balanced when we eat healthy, maintain a healthy weight and get enough exercise. It is important in the healing of PTSD for you to be committed to total body wellness. Physically releasing energy along with eating right can be powerful steps in making life more livable with PTSD.

My rule of thumb is if nature made it, then it's real food and the best for your body. PTSD can create a disassociation with your body so it is so important to eat healthy whenever possible and don't forget to eat! The better your diet, PTSD symptoms should be easier to manage.

With PTSD we often tend to push feelings and sensations away to keep ourselves safe. In this mindset you are only concerned with your immediate safety. Emotions are not considered important if your body is thinking it is facing life or death. Taking a conscious moment to connect and breathe is important for you physically and mentally. This will give you the ability to listen to your body for a moment.

If you take a short break to connect with your body, these moments of breathing will help to calm your nervous system. The more breathing breaks you incorporate into your day will soon become a habit. Taking short breathing breaks can also make you aware of when you may need to take longer breaks. Deep breathing and connection to self is important for everyone whether they have PTSD or not. It can be a hard skill to learn but will get easier the more you try.

Your commitment to self must be there. If you can become more aware of your body, you will be more connected to your thoughts as well. Being aware of all sensations and feelings are good for PTSD sufferers. Continually being stuck in fight-flight-fawn-or-freeze mode can numb you from emotions, physical needs and situational awareness. Deep belly breathing breaks will help ease this urgency the more you practice. Give yourself grace to tell yourself you are safe even when your body doesn't feel it. Give yourself grace to take a break.

Being physically healthy is a great way to combat PTSD. I don't recommend any form of exercise more than another. It is important you find something you enjoy and you're moving your body! Becoming your best version of yourself and respecting yourself is a huge step in showing yourself love and healing your nervous system from the damages of PTSD. Don't give up on health! If you take care of your health, your body will take care of you!

I hope you slowly learn to be comfortable with restful moments during the day. Remember to eat healthy and exercise! Go get it! Your health is important—mentally, physically and spiritually.

Key Points:

Health should be addressed on four levels; mentally, physically, spiritually and socially.

Striving for health and balance on a physical level can kick start your mental health.

Taking care of your physical body will only enhance and speed up your mental health progress.

Exercise has so many benefits. It is important to incorporate it into your lifestyle when striving for mental health clarity.

CHAPTER 9

SERVICE DOGS

Having a Service Dog can be a beautiful healing tool. Service Dogs are amazing medical equipment for individuals with PTSD. I have seen firsthand through the nonprofit I created (Servcie Dog Strong) how beneficial SD's are for Sexual Assault Survivors. Animals in general and therapy animals in particular are helpful for people affected with trauma, but this chapter is specifically about Service dogs.

Animals can create a special bond with people, especially people who have experienced trauma. The animal connection is safe for trauma victims. It can be very hard to reestablish a safe connection with another person when you have experienced great trauma. Animals, service dogs and therapy animals can be a safer and more comfortable way to create a positive connection. The connection can be life changing and easily and quickly established with the right dog or animal.

I was so blessed to have been a contributor to the book, *"Animal Assisted Therapy Use Application By Condition,"* edited by Eric Altshuler. The book introduces cutting edge medical research and information on service dogs and animal therapy for use with many conditions, not only PTSD. It propels the research on animal assisted therapies to a new level. It is the first book with evidence that goes in depth about service animals. Please check it out if you're interested in furthering your knowledge on service/therapy animals. This book is also a wonderful resource if you are considering your own service dog.

https://www.elsevier.com/books/animal-assisted-therapy-use-application-by-condition/altschuler/978-0-323-98815-5

Dogs are non-biased animals. They are non-judgmental quiet supporters and right there by your side. Service dogs are such a great match with SA Survivors because not only do dogs provide tactile calming effects to the handler's system, they provide emotional support when the dog is in tune with the handler. As a child and as an adult, I found the company of animals a great comfort. My love for dogs led me to start my nonprofit, **Service Dog Strong. My service dog Gunnar has helped me push through my PTSD to achieve many accomplishments that I didn't think would be possible.** Service dogs are not for everyone with PTSD. Sometimes an emotional support dog is all the person needs. There are differences between Service Dogs and ESA's, so please research and find what is best for you and your lifestyle.

I began *Service Dog Strong* (SDS) with only a dream. I was a stay-at-home mother with no extra financial resources. My dream was to provide service dogs to sexual assault survivors and MST (Military Sexual Trauma survivors). Just as Gunnar took my recovery to the next level, I wanted that help for others. I knew firsthand that dogs could hold the key to a special kind of healing. I knew that if a combat Veteran found a service dog helpful, then of course anyone else with PTSD could find help from having a service dog. All I knew was we had to make a connection 'a thing.'

When I was in the Army, I was violently sexually assaulted. This trauma left me with PTSD and a TBI (Traumatic Brain Injury). When I reached out for help and got my service dog, my life changed for the better. My anxiety lessened, I was able to go out in public with confidence and all my PTSD symptoms showed improvement. I learned that most nonprofits only provided service dogs to combat veterans and no other forms of PTSD sufferers.

I set out on a journey to overcome my PTSD. Along the way I would try to help others as I was fortunate enough to have been helped by a lonely shelter dog turned superhero service dog. I started SDS in 2019, and since then have been steadily trying to raise awareness on the healing connection between sexual assault survivors and service dogs. In a community where so many survivors of sexual assault need help, using a shelter dog that needs a home is a perfect fit. Service dogs are being proven to be a very important tool, and medical equipment, to help in the treatment of PTSD no matter what trauma caused the PTSD.

Our nonprofit ran survivor group classes, overseen by a professional dog trainer, teaching how to train their dogs for their personal needs. It is important the survivor is committed to the daily task of knowing how to handle the dog and personally train them, so the dog doesn't forget their training. This training is helpful for the survivor allowing them direct involvement in their recovery and the ability to teach their dog new tasks later on if needed.

The nonprofit was one of the first in the nation to directly help MST survivors. However, service dogs are not for everyone and can come with their own issues. Dogs can be a huge commitment financially and to your lifestyle. So please do your research before getting a service dog.

Being married to a combat veteran who was diagnosed with PTSD, and me being diagnosed with SA-PTSD, I was able to see firsthand how our symptoms overlapped. You can experience difficulty in crowds, distrust with authority and others, being isolated or always engaging in risky or adrenalin-seeking behaviors. Addictive behaviors and self-medicating to numb feelings are common reactions for people dealing with PTSD. Even happy or joyful feelings can be harder to handle and experience.

Anger can come easily, while other emotions are harder to express. Anger is such a primal emotion that it can become the 'go-to' emotion for PTSD sufferers. People with PTSD often cannot express their limits and boundaries. Often the limits have not been established so others in their life get the kick back from when the limits have been crossed unknowingly. It can be easier to isolate than to break out of a comfort zone and try to socialize.

Service dogs can help to even out emotions and to bring joy to a person dealing with depression. Just the act of petting an animal can create positive new neural-pathways in the brain. Tactile stimulation can be healing and calming. A service dogs can provide support in public by helping to encourage individuals with PTSD to socialize more comfortably.

Reflecting back on the long journey and the obstacles I went through with PTSD symptoms, there were years I didn't even know I had PTSD. I walked around jaded and masked my anxiety. Today, I can enjoy being around thousands of people or I can enjoy being alone. I have overcome many triggers and have fun without always thinking of my past. Gunner helped facilitate this for me. I have gotten to the point where I don't need him in many situations anymore.

I used to walk around thinking everyone could see my PTSD symptoms. The reality is no one can see if you have PTSD from the outside. No one can tell what you have been through unless you show them by the way you behave or act. Owning a service dog shows the public that you have a disability. This is something you must consider when thinking about whether a service dog would be beneficial to you or not.

Having my service dog by my side was a huge help in readjusting my comfort level when in public and helping me stay in the present moment. Gunner helped me remain calm in many situations and helped me check in with myself by having him by my side. Gunner brought love and light into my condition. Gunner gave me confidence. He was so helpful, yet I did not want to be fully reliant on him for the rest of my life. I was ready to learn the skills I needed with one service dog and was not looking to have to keep training other SD's once he passed. My thinking was that having a service dog as a helping hand would not be a forever life raft. My service dog is just a tool that I am in charge of. Hence, I was in charge, not the dog. As much as we like to give all the credit to the dogs, the real credit goes to the handler for teaching and maintaining the dog. I knew I would do this on my own one day. I eventually started going out on my own.

Having a service dog does bring direct attention to your unseen disability. The general public- (and even many professionals), is unaware or ignorant of proper ADA laws and service dog etiquette. This can be an opportunity to sharpen interpersonal skills and help inform the public about service dogs. This can also be very frustrating when you are out living your life and not wanting to be bothered at times. It is not your responsibility to inform the public or businesses on the laws or that they are not allowed to pet your service dog. You will definitely encounter this when you own a service dog and will have to be prepared to handle these situations.

The amount of confidence and skills I learned by having Gunner is immense. The help I received was what drove me to want to help make service dogs available to others. Service dogs can be life changing, yet, please keep in mind they are a lifetime of commitment, at least for the life of the dog. Service dogs are not the only solution to PTSD, so please weigh your options carefully. You will be caring for this animal. In turn the animal will care for you. It is a beautiful combination in my opinion, but not to be taken lightly or to think that the dog will do all the work for you. The dog is your responsibility. This in turn teaches you that you can be in control of your life and your PTSD symptoms.

Key Points:

Service Dogs can be an amazing benefit to people with PTSD.

Service Dogs are not for everyone and need to be properly vetted. Please do your research before deciding if one is right for you.

Service Dogs are different from Emotional Support animals thus finding the right fit will be different for each individual's lifestyle.

Service Dogs require a lot of research and care before deciding to add a SD to your life.

You are the one in control of your dog, thus you are the one in control of your life.

CHAPTER 10

Transcendental Meditation

The Transcendental Meditation ® technique (TM) is a distinct form of meditation. I found TM to be so effective at calming my mind, I will never do another type of meditation. I enjoyed and found the best results with this simple form of meditation.

Having been through many years of therapy, I have had many counselors try different, often Western forms of meditation with me. Until I took the Transcendental Meditation course, I felt that I had never truly meditated before. Even though a lot of my PTSD symptoms were manageable at that point in my life, I was experiencing sleep difficulties. I had trouble falling asleep and trouble staying asleep. Getting proper sleep can be essential in overcoming PTSD symptoms. A huge breakthrough came when I got a full night's rest the first night I started the TM course.

The TM course taught me an easy, effortless way to meditate and helped me sleep through the night. I recall the first night I went home from learning meditation. I went right to sleep without worry. No prescription necessary! The TM technique was the easiest meditation for me to learn and practice, compared to many other ways to meditate which I found hard to follow and ineffective at calming my mind. Other forms of meditation I tried have not been as successful. Although, please do not let it stop you from trying other types. For me, visualization, focusing on breath or listening to a guided meditation were not easy or effective ways to meditate for me, as they require more mental strain and focus than I could give. TM does not require strain or mental visualization. TM is a simple mental technique taught by a certified teacher that allows the mind to effortlessly quiet and settle. You sit down and close your eyes, follow your teacher's instructions and you will experience this simple technique that has been monumental to helping me find peace and quiet on a daily basis no matter what else is going on around me. I experienced great relief and rest from doing the TM meditation daily.

Once you learn TM you can do it by yourself. When practicing TM you don't force your mind to quiet, it happens effortlessly. This is the beauty and difference between TM and other forms of meditation. TM allows the mind to spontaneously access quieter states of awareness.

When I first practiced TM, I experienced sleepiness from doing this meditation. My system had been on full alert for many years and in doing this meditation, it finally had a chance to rest. It gave my mind and body what I needed to heal. This meditation comes highly recommended by those who have tried it all over the world. It originated in India thousands of years ago and was taught to the Beatles by Maharishi Mahesh Yogi, who then brought it to the West. It became famous in the United States in the 1970's. I will forever be grateful for this restored understanding of meditation.

This meditation is like no other I have found because it requires little effort and does not require me to focus or 'calm' myself. You come as you are. This meditation just happens easily and effectively. Over time, the longer I regularly practice the TM program, the better the results. The benefits are cumulative. Although I received amazing results the first time more and more, the peaceful state of mind is deeper and comes more quickly.

TM classes are offered for a fee and you are taught by a certified TM teacher. The 501 (c)(3) nonprofit educational organization that teaches TM technique in the US offers sliding scales based on income which is very helpful. My personal feelings over this being the perfect meditation for people with PTSD is backed by research that can be found on the TM.org website. "TM technique reduces symptoms of PTSD and depression by 20.5 percent." There was a 20.5 percent reduction in psychological distress in military personnel after practicing TM. "One study showed that the Transcendental Meditation technique decreased the need for psychotropic medications required for anxiety and PTSD management and increased psychological well-being." In

PTSD AND WHAT HELPED ME

2024 there was a groundbreaking study that found TM to be most effective at treating PTSD compared to other forms of meditation. The study can be found here: https://www.eurekalert.org/news-releases/1068462

Because TM is so simple to learn, anyone can enjoy it. Even children can learn this meditation and it is taught in some schools.

Adding a daily meditation practice can highly advance your mental and physical health. Struggling with other forms of meditation left me jaded and wanting to give up on meditation altogether. I often thought it was stupid and something someone like me would never learn to meditate because I had too much trauma and I find it hard to focus at times. The pure beauty of the TM technique is that it does not require you to hyper focus. You don't force anything. I come out of 20 minutes of TM feeling like I have slept for 20 hours. I am so relieved to have found this simple and effective meditation after struggling with other forms of meditation that left me more aggravated than before I sat down to meditate. TM is the real deal! More information and where to sign up to learn TM can be found on TM.org. The David Lynch Foundation offers scholorships for first responders, soldiers, Veterans and sexual assault survivors to learn the TM technique, please visit their site to learn more and apply: https://www.resilient-warriors.org/ https://www.davidlynchfoundation.org/

Key Points:

TM has been scientifically proven to help with PTSD and mental health symptoms.

TM has been the easiest and most beneficial form of mediation I have found.

TM requires little effort and once learned in a short course, you can practice for a lifetime.

CHAPTER 11

Martial Arts

Practicing in a martial arts class can be healing. Martial arts enhance mental stability and character building alongside physical fitness.

My healing journey wouldn't be complete without a whole chapter devoted to martial arts and Taekwondo. Martial arts encompasses the special values of the mind, body and spirit. Health is found in more than just in the mind and body, your spirit needs to be fulfilled as well. Martial arts taught me not only mental and physical wellness, but the love for the sport made my spirit happy. While I have practiced Taekwondo, Muya Thai and MMA, I believe all forms of martial arts hold their own benefits and it is all a personal choice which type of martial arts that you try.

I didn't find out how great martial arts can be until I decided to take my son to Taekwondo. I was looking for a sport my young son could participate in. When we went to the first class, I saw whole families practicing, from 4 years old to grandparents. My son was getting use to the class and I would watch from the sidelines. He did so well and I was so proud of him. My PTSD and anxiety kept me from not wanting to try it, although learning to kick and punch looked like a fun way to destress and get exercise. I eventually chose to push my fears aside and lead by example, hoping my daughter would join if she saw me alongside her brother.

Joining a class with others was intimidating. Trying new things where you are bound to fail and look silly at times is hard for anyone, PTSD or not. My desire to show my kids a healthy lifestyle propelled me to overcome some anxiety about being in a class with other students. Going 'for the kids' took some pressure off the whole public scenario. But, to my surprise, I ended up loving Taekwondo for myself! I found a new, healthy hobby and lifestyle from those weekly lessons. It is my hope that by sharing my journey in martial arts, you can find strength as a survivor through some form of self-defense or martial arts classes. It can be empowering and fun. I must give my kids thanks for getting me hooked on this beautiful form of exercise and personal development.

My daughter ended up enrolling with me and my oldest son. The baby was too young to attend at the time. Martial arts brought our family together through fitness and discipline. It taught us all confidence, respect and was a fun activity we all could do.

Becoming physically stronger and more in tune with my body was a very calming experience. Growing in physical power and strength, gaining confidence in learning how to defend myself. I enjoyed getting better at techniques and learning character development that was taught by the instructor of the class. Not only were you encouraged to make your best punches, you were also encouraged to be the best person you can be to others and that you are the most important person in your life.

Taekwondo not only gave me confidence, it taught me new social skills. We practiced more than throwing blocks and kicks, we also learned meditation and public speaking. Our teacher taught us not to panic in stressful situations, which was very valuable for me and my PTSD. Taekwondo is about your mental state just as much as your physical state.

I felt powerful and strong in class. Taekwondo quickly became a new healthy obsession. I loved the fact that I was becoming more in shape as well. Doing something physical is so important for PTSD healing. It created a bond between my children and me as we practiced at home getting ready to test for our newest belts.

Physical activity can release negative energy from the body as well as releasing endorphins *(endorphins are the body's natural painkillers and create a general feeling of well-being)*. The action of punching and kicking the air or bag was freeing for me as a survivor. It strengthened the mind and body connection as well as balancing both the right and left sides of the body. Regaining balance and coordination was very helpful for me too. Better posture and balance improvement is improved with a martial arts practice.

Martial arts can be an amazing form of 'therapy.' It helps bring awareness to the world and people around you. It strengthens the mind-body connections. It helped me learn to be more comfortable around people. I learned to focus more on tasks at hand rather than my fears, insecurities and onlookers. It takes commitment and humility to try something new. It is a healthy, humbling experience learning new things in front of others. Don't let this deter you as the beauty of an interactive class is that everyone else is learning alongside you and you're not the only one making mistakes.

Taekwondo made me feel powerful, strong, and alive. The classes added to my ability to maintain a healthy lifestyle. Your body and your mind hold onto pain. Engaging in some form of physical activity is very beneficial in the healing process. Almost anyone can start some type of martial arts program. Taekwondo, especially, is a very low impact form of martial arts. Karate, Jujutsu or tai chi are just a few of the other forms of martial arts available. Some are high impact while there are other forms more suitable if you have injuries and need low impact.

I was blown away at how good the children were with their practice, reciting memorized paragraphs, and their devotion to the sport. As an adult it was a beautifully humbling experience to see a five year old kick better than you! It gave me a mission to set goals for myself and do my best. Physical activity does release chemicals like endorphins and oxytocin, often called the 'love hormone,' which plays a role in establishing emotional bonds and boosting your mood. It gave me the same happy feelings, but achieved in a healthy way.

Taekwondo focuses a lot on improving your character alongside physical improvement. The mind and body and social connections are emphasized. It led me to make changes in my life, even to the point of putting myself first, (which is very difficult for moms). Every belt that I obtained was a boost of self-confidence. A job well done and well earned. It was such a good feeling to see my kids earn belts and together and it was one of the proudest moments of my life to share this amazing experience with them.

The public speaking portion of the class helped me get over the fear of speaking in front of people. In class, we memorized paragraphs and recited them in front of the class. I never wanted to be in the public eye, talk on camera, or speak about one of the most traumatizing moments of my life. But- I ended up doing all this to help others and share my story. Class helped me gain confidence and I learned to speak more direct and powerfully. Public speaking is a big accomplishment for someone who has experienced PTSD and I gained a lot of experience in class.

Through my training, I learned to rewrite my body's response system to threats. It is so important to practice reacting and calming down your response to stress. For SA Survivors, self-defense classes or martial arts classes can be life changing. Martial arts classes, personal protection, self-defense can empower a Survivor. Learning how to properly use force can physically and mentally put you in power. Not to mention that the simple acts of kicking and punching can help physically relieve stress. These classes have been so beneficial for my life personally, physically and in business. I highly recommend finding the right martial arts class that most suits you.

I want to give a big shout out to my martial arts teachers Master Park, Miss Demi, Nostos and Manny!

Key Points:

Martial arts can be a fun way to incorporate healing and physical fitness into your healing journey.

Since emotions are stored in the body, such programs accelerate PTSD healing by creating awareness of the body, mind and spirit simultaneously.

There are enough forms of Martial arts available where anyone can find a class that properly fits their physical stamina level, age and physical ability.

CHAPTER 12

DIFFERENT THERAPIES

The following is an exhaustive list with description and overview of therapies available for PTSD.

The medical community has started to research PTSD more and there seems to be appropriate awareness increasing over its severity. PTSD has been documented in literature since Homer, so it is about time we break the stigma of mental illness and find solutions. I suggest trying a mixture of options till you find the best one that you can maintain. Having the idea that you are already healed as an individual and just need help processing your trauma can remove the guilt and shame. PTSD can be a natural reaction when experiencing trauma, so there is nothing wrong with you. Your trauma happened to you. It is NOT who you are. Learning new ways to communicate and operate in a healthy manner should be your goal. A reduction of stress and anxiety can come the more you focus on your strengths, future goals and take actions to improve your future.

Being open to different therapies is important to find which will work for you. I will touch upon some of the therapies I have tried or heard about. This is a diversified but not a complete listing. These suggestions are presented for educational purposes only. Be sure to consult your medical and mental healthcare team along your journey. This list includes traditional and non-traditional therapies. Be open enough to seek some benefit from everything you try, even if you try something that may not be the right fit. I believe you set the tone for progress. If you go into therapy thinking your trauma is too big to move and get past, no therapy is going to work for you.

I wanted to try everything I could to get the help I needed. I tried the traditional and non-traditional routes. I tried alternative therapies to find my healing and traditional western modalities. The purpose of therapy is to uncover your past trauma in order to process it in a safe environment. Confronting past trauma can be intimidating and re-traumatizing. The alternative is never dealing with the pain, so I do believe it will eventually get easier. If you have a true yearning to overcome and grow, then I believe you will see progress no matter how small it may be. Put in an honest effort and participate for numerous sessions before thinking about giving up.

EMDR (Eye Movement Desensitization and Reprocessing)

This was a very powerful therapy I tried. It was intense. EMDR therapy released me from so much guilt I was holding onto. It brought me back to moments in the military I had blocked out. Some of the memories that were revealed freed me but were also very hard to re-process. Through this therapy I did relive a lot of the trauma I had suppressed. Overall, I do feel this was beneficial even though at times, it was quite difficult to go through. EMDR brought out good and bad memories. The help came faster than conventional talk therapy could. I do highly recommend this therapy to those with PTSD.

Stellate Ganglion Nerve Block Therapy

This is a new therapy that has had some great results for some while others have not noticed huge changes. It is a short procedure that can have lasting effects of relief. Some may need the procedure repeated. The beauty of this therapy is that it has little down time and does not require ongoing attention. It does not require you to confront emotions dealing with PTSD or your trauma.

A stellate ganglion block is a short medical procedure where a doctor injects local anesthetic (numbing medicine) into the sympathetic nerves located on either side of the voice box in your neck area. The injection numbs and can calm down the fight or flight reaction. The length of time that the results work is different for each person. Some may need a few procedures, or it could take one to "reset" your system. This is a procedure for PTSD that doesn't require "therapy" or long hours of work. For this reason, I feel it could really benefit some or work well in combination with other forms of therapy.

Group Therapy

It can be very helpful to create comrade connections and to safely ease into human interactions. Being with others who have been through the same things as you and sharing with one another can be healing. Group therapy can create the affirmation you are not alone and can help you understand that what you have been dealing with and feeling is quite real. You might end up making a new best friend as well. Open yourself to a new experience and get what you give.

Working in group therapy allows you to pace yourself at your own comfort level. Don't make friends if you don't want to. Listen to their stories and share your own. Try to focus on your future goals rather than making it a pity party. Maybe you can get something out of it, but you won't know until you give it an honest try for a while. You could choose to stay at home alone and suffer more in your own head. The choice is yours.

Service Dogs (SD) or Emotional Support Animal (ESA)

I love the use of service dogs for the reduction of PTSD symptoms. ESA's can also be beneficial. SD's and ESA's are different from one another. ESA's are different from SD's in that ESA's cannot be taken in public, and SD's are allowed in public spaces. SD's are highly trained and chosen for their nonreactivity to noises and distractions, and thus can be taken in public facilities. These spaces include but are not limited to: commercial facilities, private businesses, medical offices, public transportation, airlines and commercial buildings. SD's need hundreds of hours of training to maintain their socially acceptable behavior and to be trained medically for what the handler needs. They must act accordingly in public as well as being attentive to their handler.

Taking care of a dog is a lot of work, whether you bring them in public or they stay at home. SD's require more effort as they need extra grooming and daily training to be acceptable in public and comfortable around all circumstances that could arise, such as loud noises or elevators. Service dogs can be taken into restaurants and grocery stores, so they must be kept extra clean. Daily training is required when owning a service dog to ensure their proper behavior out in public. ESA's do not require special training. They are more for emotional comfort to their owner and do not provide any medical assistance training. ESA's can be a good choice if you don't have the time to devote to intense training and don't need medical help in public.

Service dogs are NOT for those who are in the early healing stages of PTSD. If you are unable to take care of yourself and have no motivation due to depression, then adding the care of an animal might not be the best fit at that moment.

Dogs (SD OR ESA) need to be taken care of like a child. The handler needs to be able to provide proper care for the animal on a consistent basis even in the midst of a PTSD panic attack. The handler needs to be able to function on basic levels enough to walk and feed the dog daily. You will need to be able to care for the dog financially, have adequate space and also other family members you might live with need to be accepting of a dog. When in public, with your   SD, your disability will be amplified. Your 'unseen' disability will now be seen. This can be added attention not everyone is ready for.

A service dog also is meant to help push yourself to do things you previously did not do. Service dogs can help you go out in public places or help you get back into the workplace. Although there are ADA laws in America that protect disabled persons and their service dogs, still many employers and businesses do not follow these laws out of ignorance. You will become a teacher of ADA laws and disability rights information, whether you like it or not. The general public does not understand service dog etiquette. You will have strangers come up and pet your dog as if they were like any other pet instead of a working dog. Or you may be harassed for having your service dog when people don't understand the difference between pets and service dogs. Take this into consideration when determining if you need an ESA or SD.

If you are interested in more information on service dogs, therapy animals or ESA's, I highly recommend you read the following book, <u>Animal Assisted Therapy Use Application by Condition</u>, edited by Eric Altschuler, published by Elsevier.

I wrote Chapter 8 on *Sexual Assault and Service Dogs*. This groundbreaking book contains the most up-to-date, medically studied and comprehensive data on animal-assisted therapy. In reading this book you can learn which type of assistance animal is best for you.

https://shop.elsevier.com/books/animal-assisted-therapy-use-application-by-condition/altschuler/978-0-323-98815-5

Prolonged Exposure Therapy

This therapy can be done with a therapist or on your own. It is done by journaling your story and trauma and re-reading it repeatedly on a daily or weekly basis. The point is to desensitize yourself to your story and not have it be as alarming or traumatic anymore. You will be facing head on your memories of the traumatic events. Personally, I started this therapy before I decided to start *Service Dogs Strong*. My heart was so full of joy when I got Gunnar and was able to take him in public that I wanted to share my story in hopes of helping other survivors.

I chose to tell my story in a 'crowdfunding' post. I talked a while with my therapist before making the post. We decided that in order for me to get ready to share my story via the internet, exposure therapy would be a good way to get me ready. The post ended up catching the attention of local media and I was able to raise the thousands needed to legally incorporate Service Dog Strong. In sharing my story publicly, I had to be comfortable sharing and reading it over and over to myself in private. The more I shared my story, the easier it became, although never less painful. It is up to you whether you decide to share your story publicly or not, but writing it down and reading it to yourself is a good start to healing.

Exposure therapy is very beneficial in the long run but can also cause discomfort. This therapy should be completed when you have support and a therapist to be able to dissect any emotions that will arise.

Inner child healing work

This is vital to any recovery work. To truly get to the bottom of who you are and why you respond to situations the way you do, speaking love and acceptance to your inner child is vital. You can work with a therapist to do inner child healing work or start on your own.

You can always explore healing your inner child and any childhood trauma you may have gone through on your own by journaling. I wrote my childhood self a letter. I wrote everything I would have wanted to hear as a child. I wrote to her all the things that she needed to hear at the time. I told her she was safe and going to be ok and the trauma was not her fault. I healed myself and was there for myself,-- healing myself across time and space. It can be very fulfilling and help to bring closure. This can become a triggering mechanism just as any therapy can potentially be, depending on the amount of trauma from your childhood. The more traumas you unpack, the lighter you will feel once you have chosen to be that brave adult you needed when you were a child.

Inner child healing work needs to be done to truly move into the healed person you need to be to overcome PTSD. Let your therapist know that you want to explore your inner child. Speak gentle words of healing to your inner child and forgive yourself. Only you know what you needed as a child and what you needed to hear. This work can be a wonderful way of learning more about yourself and starting your healing process. Talk to the hurt child within you and convey words of peace and comfort.

Speaking to your inner child in a safe environment can be healing to your past and the adult you are now. Choosing to avoid childhood trauma will just push it down further bringing volcanic anger to the surface and creating an environment for the pain to remain. Hard inner work will bring results.

This method allowed me to place healing in my own hands. It brought me into a stronger mindset, rather than remaining the victim. This therapy can also bring up much discomfort, but keep in mind that the discomfort and painful memories will pass. In its place you will receive grace to process the memories and alleviate this pain in the future.

Traditional talk therapy

Find yourself a counselor! Find a psychologist! Find a spiritual counselor! Or all of them! Get outside of your head and talk about it! Don't keep it all in. You're only going to keep feeling the same way if you continue to hold onto those awful feelings and not allow them to process through your mind, body and soul. Eventually you can come to a safe place where you are ready to release them. Thank yourself for the memories and their lessons. The feelings and responses to them were there to keep you safe at the time. Now you no longer need to hold onto the past and those unhealthy behaviors. Now you no longer have any use from the old behaviors and are ready to embrace your future progress.

It will take time and patience. You can still do it! You deserve happiness and inner healing. You deserve a new happy life and new happy feelings. I have found such success and life improvement from my therapy sessions. I will always choose to be in therapy no matter if I am dealing with difficult life issues or not. I think of therapy as my insurance to maintain my mental health. Not a red flag that something is wrong with me. I have found that the healthiest people are in therapy and it's the mentally unstable and unhealthy people who avoid necessary therapy.

I believe everyone should be in therapy for a time. My therapist helped to enhance my life immensely. Most people have been through some sort of trauma, but therapy isn't only for those who have been through traumatic experiences. It can be used to stay mentally healthy. We go to the doctor to check up on our physical health, so why shouldn't we all have the same regular mental checkups?

My therapy schedule differed in frequency based on what was going on in my life and how long I had been attending sessions. When I first enrolled in therapy, I went weekly. I had a lot to discuss and a strong desire to quickly get the inner work done. As I progressed and found some peace, I eventually moved to monthly sessions. Therapy can be what you make it. If you are just trying to be the best person you can be and don't have childhood trauma to work on, then your sessions can be as needed. If you have a lot of stressors in life, even though it may be hard to find the time to devote to yourself, therapy can be vitally important.

Stay mentally healthy! I optimistically imagine a world where everyone has been to therapy and has learned safe, healthy ways to communicate and interact peacefully with others. Therapy has really helped keep me in check, helped me feel my best and treat others with the best intentions possible.

Talking about things that happen with a neutral party can be helpful. It can take a while to find the right therapist for your personality. With the option of online therapy, you have a greater chance of finding one that works for you than just being tied down to your local area. A good therapist should be there to encourage you but also push you gently to explore hard issues as you progress. If your therapist is not knowledgeable about your particular situation, (i.e., systematic oppression or cultural experiences), they can potentially miss something that could help you or cause more trauma by ignoring the trauma you are living through.

Please choose your therapist with care. If they are not helping you progress, then it is your responsibility to find a new therapist. Therapists should not be telling you what you want to hear, but gently guiding you to do the hard internal work necessary for you to find inner peace. Therapists should also not remain silent; you are using your time just for a venting session. Your therapist should be giving you feedback,- when necessary, but you also need to speak up and set guidelines on what you expect to get out of therapy. They should assess how you learn and respond best to constructive criticism. Ask the hard questions and allow your therapist to give you honest feedback so that you don't stagnate in therapy. Be open to making improvements.

I believe most of my sessions were uncomfortable. I cried a lot. Maybe this is why a lot of people avoid therapy. There needs to come a point in life when you are ready to let all the baggage go. Once I got through the first few years of diving deep into what was bothering me and examining my past, things got easier. For me, therapy became a safe zone for my week. Therapy was a happy place where I could talk freely and feel connected to another human being who had my best future in mind.

I was really blessed to have some good counselors. There were also some that I really just didn't vibe with. After a time of trying to progress, I have had to ask certain counselors to change how the sessions worked, or to ask them for more feedback. It can be nerve racking to "fire" your counselor, but if you have tried different methods within your sessions, or you just don't feel the counselor is putting their all in your session or the right fit, then it is acceptable to try a different therapist.

If you are not putting in the inner work and really trying with your sessions, then your therapist won't be able to help you with your healing process. Never feel bad about speaking up for yourself and seeking a better connection to find healing if your therapy sessions are not helping you achieve your goals. Go as slow or fast as is comfortable. Listen to your heart and take your healing one day at a time. The longer you work in therapy, the easier it will become as you release and work through your trauma.

Releasing past trauma does not mean that your life will be happy or lucky when you are forced to live in a severely oppressive system. Capitalism preys on persons with mental illness and any population that is not within the upper-class. Keep this in mind when seeking a therapist so you can find one who understands that it can be a normal reaction to hold anger and be depressed at times when you are being unfairly treated by a highly oppressive system.

Cognitive Processing Therapy (CPT)

I tried this program with my counselor at the Vet Center. It was very straightforward and easy to get through. It consists of a workbook that you review each week. You will have some homework to finish after your session as well. It teaches you to see how you are currently viewing situations in your world and how to change what needs changing. My view and self-belief of the world going into CPT was that the world is not safe,- and people cannot be trusted. These facts for me were strongly felt before I started CPT. What CPT did was to direct more of my attention to other instances in my life that were safe and that there in fact were some situations in my life where people did

NOT take advantage of me. My view of reality changed to a more softened view after CPT. A life view where it can be safe and unsafe at times.

CPT helped me to keep both sides of these 'facts' in the forefront of my mind. It helped me balance my inner beliefs toward being more encompassing and positive. CPT helped me combat my negative inner beliefs. When I felt fear or anger, I would visit it with bravery and see exactly what I was telling myself. Then like a journalist, analyze those inner thoughts to see if they were justified or coming from a place of trauma as a default negative pattern. I was able to rationalize my fears and see the truth. I was usually able to put the old 'facts' I felt to rest and explain to myself:

"Yes, the world can be a scary, unsafe place, but I am different today. I am strong and aware. Bad things may happen, but more good things tend to happen. I am more aware and more prepared. I know how to keep myself safe. I do not need to fear things that have not happened. I do not need to put more energy into my fears, making them statistically happen more often by feeding the fear. I am going to feed a different view of what might happen. I am going to think of something positive happening. Maybe I will meet a friend instead. Maybe, I can be happy! Maybe I can even bless someone today instead of sitting around and waiting for something bad to happen to me! I can create greatness and peace in my life instead of waiting for it to find me. I can trust my higher power. I can trust my strength and the things I

learned from my life. I can choose to be happy today. If something does go wrong, as it often can, I can trust that I will be brave enough to handle it with grace and that all problems hold many solutions. Bad things do happen, and we cannot always stop them. But good has always come from all the adversity I have been through. I am a survivor, and I will keep surviving."

Light Therapy (Phototherapy)

This uses artificial light to help regulate the body more effectively. It can help increase serotonin and help sleep cycles, anxiety and pain management

Occupational Therapy

Seeing an OT can be very beneficial as they can assist in sensory processing, emotional regulation, social skills, coping skills and connect you with other support professionals. They help with the functional difficulties PTSD can pose and offer hands-on support.

Physical Therapy

This can be beneficial to gradually help reintroduction to physical movement and strength exercises. This focuses on physical symptoms and helps with overall wellness.

Narrative Exposure Therapy

This therapy is specifically designed for individuals with CPTSD or those who have experienced multiple traumatic events. It can be provided by social workers, therapists or psychologists. This therapy has the individual create a narrative of their entire life with understanding and less focused on the traumatic events as a whole.

Hypnosis

This is a treatment that can be done in a few sessions. I have not personally tried this, but this can be an option for some who are seeking alternative therapies with minimal side effects.

Tai Chi/Martial Arts

I love adding physical movement to recovery because it is proven that exercise is just as important to recovery as the mental aspect of traumatic healing. Martial arts incorporate valuable skills in movement, focus and self-discipline. These skills can be invaluable to someone with PTSD and greatly beneficial.

Tapping

This is an easy modality to learn and involves simple tapping movements on pressure points on the body that speed relaxation and calm down PTSD symptoms. It can be done anywhere and anytime as it just involves you tapping certain

DIFFERENT THERAPIES

areas of your body and is surprisingly very effective and calming. The longer you practice tapping, the easier your body will return to a calm state. Tapping can be taught to children so it is a therapy that anyone can try.

Yoga

Try any of the many forms of yoga and you're bound to find progress with PTSD symptoms and a new positive addiction! One of my favorite forms of yoga is laughter yoga. This is quite different from your traditional hatha yoga, but laughter yoga has classes and groups just as hatha or hot yoga does. Laughter yoga is fun and releases a lot of tension in the body and mind. I would encourage everyone to seek and try out different forms until you find your match. There is a yoga type for any physical plane you are on. My personal favorite is Kundalini yoga.

Yoga not only helps the body but also helps calm the mind which is so helpful for us with PTSD.

Massage/Bodywork

Getting a massage can promote health, relaxation and release deep seated trauma in the body, if one is ready. My recommendation as a certified massage therapist is to get on a consistent schedule. The more the body feels a positive touch, the more it will be comfortable with relaxing. This will help to ease your PTSD symptoms on both a physical and mental level (since both are intertwined). Trauma is not only held in

119

the mind, but there are spots in the body that directly relate to trauma you have endured.

When your body and mind are ready to release your trauma, it can be a monumental step. It took me getting weekly massages for months to finally feel a sense of release. Massage schools also offer discounted massages from students if you are on a budget.

Reiki

This modality can be given by direct touch and hands on, or without any contact. This being said it is perfect for those SA and PTSD survivors who are not comfortable with touch, and the Reiki is just as effective. It is very effective and goes hand in hand with massage and bodywork or can be done on its own. People with PTSD have seen great relaxation and reduction of symptoms from Reiki and its proven to be good for anxiety, pain relief and speeds up healing. I became Reiki certified and now I can perform Reiki on myself as well as others. nIt is a very gentle technique I highly recommend.

Micro-dosing of Mushrooms (Psilocybin)

This is an exciting therapy that is being studied and will be available to everyone without jail time for those seeking recovery soon I hope. Mushrooms are natural and have been used for centuries for self-discernment and healing. The expanded uses of traditional ancient medicine are being shown to have extremely promising results in mental health. Micro-dosing needs to be done with care and with a care provider who can provide the right dose. As with any medicine, it is not for everyone. I have experienced great awakenings and true feelings of peace when taking small doses of mushrooms. They have positively enhanced my life by helping me move through trauma and move past a lot of social anxiety. I recommend using mushrooms sparingly or just for spiritual ceremonies. I hope more medical research is done on mushrooms and laws are eliminated to create safe spaces and acceptance for other natural forms of recovery.

DMT (Dimethyltryptamine) Therapy

This assisted therapy is done under the guidance of a mental health professional and has seen impressive results in some, but not all, as is the case in any therapy. It can be done in an outpatient setting and only takes a short time. The frequency is determined by your care team. Do your research and don't be afraid to try new treatments that are becoming available.

Community involvement and Volunteering

Choosing to spend some of your time in the community helping others can be very beneficial and essential to recovery. It will take you away from your personal issues for a time and connect you with others in the community and possibly connect you to new friends and new resources. Although it may be uncomfortable at the start, it will boost your self-esteem and make you feel connected and needed. There are many opportunities to volunteer either with people or animals! Community involvement can ensure your prolonged success by giving your life a new purpose to stay sober and healthy. Also, mentoring someone who has been through a similar situation as you can be healing but can motivate you to be your best. It can provide you with a sense of accomplishment adding a glimmer of positive meaning to the trauma you have endured. Getting involved in the community, whether it be a local church, sports team, a book club or volunteer organization can often be the missing last step in feeling better after trauma. Our trauma can isolate us. Stepping outside to share human connection is vital to wellbeing and happiness. Do not skip this step. Caring connections are imperative to healing.

Ketamine Therapy

The FDA has approved ketamine for the use of treating depression, PTSD, anxiety, chronic pain and other issues. This treatment is done under a medical provider's care and has been very effective for many.

Cognitive Behavioral Conjoint therapy

This is merely cognitive therapy (*relating to the process of acquiring knowledge and understanding through thought, experience, and the senses*) but for couples/partners. It can address PTSD for one or two people who have PTSD. It is also beneficial if one person has PTSD and the other does not. If you live with someone who has PTSD, you will need support.

Neurofeedback Therapy

This can be beneficial for those who haven't responded well to traditional therapies. In this technique you learn to train your brain to manage emotions in real time by providing current brainwave activity.

Pharmaceutical Medication

There are many medications available today that treat and help manage symptoms of PTSD. Please consult your licensed doctor or psychologist to be prescribed properly.

Mindfulness Stress Reduction Therapy

These programs are structured and offered at many healthcare facilities. They encompass awareness and present moment grounding often in a group setting.

Acupuncture

Acupuncture is a traditional Chinese medicine that uses very small needles inserted in specific chi lines on the body. These are specifically chosen for an individual's ailments and concerns. Although somewhat invasive, the needles are so small it isn't painful and can be deeply healing for emotional health as well as physically. I highly recommend this therapy, as I personally enjoy my sessions greatly.

Rehabilitation and Inpatient clinics

Taking time away from the world and responsibilities to focus on healing can be just the thing an individual with PTSD might need. Some clinics can be full time for a week up to a few months, while others can be held during the day and let you go home at night. Taking enough time to focus on your healing and being in a safe space can be life changing.

Hormone Therapy

Checking your hormones can be an added therapy you can use alongside counseling. While hormone therapy is not directly used to treat PTSD, if your hormones are out of balance it can add to your stress and thus increase PTSD symptoms.

Craniosacral Therapy

This hands-on therapy is not primarily used to treat PTSD, is an effective alternative therapy that can gently help promote stress reduction, self-healing, mind-body awareness and overall health improvements.

Cannabis or CBD Therapy

Cannabis or CBD can be used medically. Please consult a licensed medical cannabis provider for dosage and what form will work best for you. There are many forms of THC or CBD available today such as tinctures, gummies, edibles or your traditional inhalation form.

Progressive Muscle Relaxation PMR

This technique involves targeting specific muscles and helps reduce stress and anxiety.

Acceptance and Commitment Therapy ACT

This psychotherapy involves managing difficult emotions with acceptance and non judgement while incorporating actions into their life so that the individual is more in control rather than being controlled by their emotions.

Somatic Therapy

This can be very helpful in creating a connection with the body and mind. It helps the individual to be aware of their body and responses to their feelings and emotions. It has been cited as helpful for those with PTSD.

Hotlines

This is not a complete list, thus the reader is encouraged to seek out personally, organizations that directly relate to their situation or that might be available in their area.
988 Veteran Suicide crisis line
Crisis Text Line 741741

Postpartum helpline: 1-800-944-4773

National Domestic Violence Hotline 1-800-799-7233

National Deaf Domestic Violence Hotline 1-855-812-1001

National Mental health hotline 1-866-903-3787

NAMI Hotline 1-800-950-6264

National Sexual Assault Hotline 1-800-656-4673

Rape Abuse and Incest National Network 1-800-656-4673

Substance Abuse and Mental Health Services Administration 1-800-662-4357

National Brain Injury Information Center 1-800-444-6443

National Child Abuse Hotline 1-800-422-4453

Disaster Distress Helpline 1-800-985-5990

LGBTQ Hotline 1-888-843-4564

Crisis Line for Kids and Teens 1-877-968-8491

Copline- International Law Enforcement Officers Hotline 1-800-267-5463

Self-help/Self-Love

You're doing it right now! You're doing your own recovery work! Reading books, listening to positive podcasts, social media or videos can be so helpful! I have learned a lot through reading autobiographies. I don't have several lifetimes to walk in people's shoes, but I can learn from others by reading their stories. If you consciously choose to find helpful positive information, you can find it. In the same way, when you are in the pit of depression and self-pity, you can find people and posts that affirm your self-loathing and hate for the world and unjust situations.

Please be aware of what you put into your psyche. What you put in will come out. What you say will be. That's why PTSD is so hurtful. It gets you stuck in past trauma and just creates more hurt and pain over and over again. Take that uncomfortable leap by filling your mind, words and thoughts with positive healing and hope. I know your life will change for the better the longer you ingest hope and healing. Healing will come to you at the right time, so don't give up.

A breakthrough often comes when you think you are at the end of being able to handle it all. You're here for a reason. Your trauma could have taken you out. But it didn't. I was meant to be alive and so are you. Make your life yours and start taking intentional steps to heal. Take steps to think positively so the world doesn't move you. You can move your mind into what you want it to find.

Could you be comfortable with your depression? When happiness and positive experiences are foreign to you, sometimes we get comfortable with chaos. The choice is yours right now to decide to try the uncomfortable. The trauma was not your fault, but healing is up to you. Your traumatic event is over, and each day is new. I do know how living in pain and adaptive behaviors can be overwhelming. I know that taking a leap of courage and trying something different can be hard, but being positive can literally change your life.

Focus more on yourself. Learning to focus on self and doing small things each day to take care of you will help to heal

PTSD symptoms. Have you eaten today? Have you washed your face? Have you made your bed? Have you gotten a haircut recently? Have you taken breathing breaks? Have you rested when you needed to?

Self-love and self-care will benefit your healing journey and is really simple to do. It doesn't have to be about buying things. You can rub your own feet. You can make yourself a nice meal and take a long shower. Loving yourself and taking some time to slow down and care for yourself is something we often forget to do when we have PTSD. Stopping the fight/flight/fawn/freeze response for a time and caring for you on a daily basis can be a learned behavior that grows into a habit. Self-love can be learned until you truly believe it inside. Don't worry if you don't feel good enough inside to actually believe it.

As I worked through my pain and trauma, I found my heart opening up more. The guilt, shame and self-loathing were replaced with an understanding of my adaptive behaviors and I gave myself grace. The more I worked on myself through counseling, the more I saw the traumatic situations as they should be seen. I released myself from the guilt and unnecessary shame.

Taking care of yourself is what will drive you to attract love from others. Start out with baby steps and work up to a whole day just for you! We all deserve to treat ourselves with care and attention.

Peace for you my friends who are on your healing journey. Healing is possible. Keep searching for what works for you!

Key Points:

Try some of these therapies on the list! Give each try an honest shot and ample time to get used to a new routine and pass it off.

Sometimes revisiting things we have tried at different points in our life can be beneficial.

Try a combination of therapies, the point is to not give up until you find what works for you.

CHAPTER 13

YOUR NEW LIFE AWAITS

Thank you for taking this journey with me exploring such sensitive subjects as our trauma and PTSD. I hope you are left with a more exciting and happier outlook. My desire is that you have more power and knowledge in your heart to believe in yourself and heal.

Even through your pain, life is calling you to live. Not to live your old life but a new life. Change is needed. Life is calling you to live a different, more evolved, caring, and healthier life. Don't be afraid to grow out of the old habits. Create love in your life and create happiness by making positive changes. It starts with healing, then creating a better vision for your life. You can create your future no matter what happened in your past. d thoughts with counseling and then create better thoughts for a better future. You deserve it.

It took me a long time to entertain positive thoughts for myself because of all the unnecessary survivor guilt and shame and all the years of abuse and degradation. Imagining good things coming to you is exciting and not selfish. With all the trauma we have endured, why can't the next chapter in our life be a good one?

It is sometimes harder to practice forgiveness for ourselves than with others. Take a minute to forgive yourself for things you did or how you acted when you were in survival mode. You have come so far; don't let anything stop you from creating a better life for yourself now. Taking care of yourself is the first step in creating a better life.

Life will keep giving you the chance to overcome all your fears until you conquer them. The same pain will keep repeating itself if the energy has not been fully awakened. Remember you are more powerful than the trauma you have been through. You are more powerful than your pain. Take back your power by inner searching and healing.

Setting your thoughts on a goal can keep you on track. Imagine that life can be better than before. That means there is always a reason to keep moving forward.

Recovery is not a continual lateral climb. I am not at all a perfect example of recovery or would ever admit that I am completely healed from my PTSD symptoms. I had to put in years of work to be comfortable enough to speak out about what has happened to me. But what if I were to entertain the thought that I am whole? If I am healed after putting in work to recover, I do not need to live in a continual battle to 'heal.'

Work through the trauma and learn to live in a head space where you are not damaged and you are now healed. "If I had waited until I felt that I was completely "healed" or never had a bad day, then Service Dog Strong would not have been started, nor this book written. I have come to a place where I have more good days than bad and I am able to create positive changes in my life instead of negative ones.

Healing is a daily assignment that can often be a very bumpy road. Some days I feel like I have my PTSD under control and then the next day I feel like I'm not making progress. The progress in my life is due to hard work and facing the uncomfortable. It is due to continually asking for better answers and a childlike attitude to learn more about PTSD. I have made tremendous progress but always leave room for improvement and progress. I share my personal journey with you hoping that it will spark your own journey to healing, understanding yourself and how PTSD can be managed. PTSD symptoms might not ever go away fully, but I do believe you can heal to a point where you can enjoy life more.

I don't feel there are enough positive messages about PTSD in the media. We are told about how many soldiers commit suicide daily. We hear about meds for PTSD, but not about lifestyle changes. We hear mainly PTSD in combat soldiers and not about other causes such as SA or gun violence. We need to hear more about the victories, big or small.We need to acknowledge the vast number of us that experience PTSD from many different traumas and that we are not alone in this.

We need to hear that recovery is possible. Your life can come back in a new beautiful, however, different way. Recovery IS possible.

This book reviews things that helped me. If these ideas can help others, then I have done my part and completed the cycle to healing. I no longer live just to survive; I can live to help others and to thrive and enjoy my life. My wish for those reading this is for you to take the time to self-examine yourself and find your own roadmap to a better destiny. If you want change, you will have to change some things in your life. Don't be scared to be you. Let your light shine and be yourself.

I wish you peace and happiness on your journey and in your life. Thank you for letting me share my intimate journey with you all. Know you are loved. You can have a better life. Never give up and Stay Strong!

www.ingramcontent.com/pod-product-compliance
Lightning Source LLC
Chambersburg PA
CBHW070450090426
42735CB00012B/2503